190
READY-TO-USE
ACTIVITIES
THAT MAKE
ENGLISH FUN!

George Watson

Illustrated by Alan Anthony

JOSSEY-BASS
A Wiley Imprint
www.josseybass.com

Published by Jossey-Bass
A Wiley Imprint
989 Market Street, San Francisco, CA 94103-1741   www.josseybass.com

Jossey-Bass books and products are available through most bookstores. To contact Jossey-Bass directly
call our Customer Care Department within the U.S. at 800-956-7739, outside the U.S. at 317-572-3986
or fax 317-572-4002.

Jossey-Bass also publishes its books in a variety of electronic formats. Some content that appears in
print may not be available in electronic books.

ISBN: 0-7879-7886-8

FIRST EDITION
10 9 8 7 6 5 4 3 2

GEORGE WATSON

*Acknowledgments
and thanks
for your
professional support
in writing the "Hooked on Learning" series.
I've truly "hooked" up with the best crew.*

MARLENE TILFORD
Advisor

CHRISTA WATSON
Advisor

ESTHER JOHNSON
Jiffy Steno Services

ALAN ANTHONY
Illustrator

George Mason

...acknowledging thanks
and thanks
for your
professional support...
in writing the "Hooked on Learning" Series
[...] Hooked up with the

CRISTA WATSON
Advisor

MARLENE FULHORST
Editor

ALAN ANTHONY
Illustrator

ESTHER JOHNSON
Jiffy Steno Services

ABOUT THE AUTHOR

George Watson (B.A., University of Saskatchewan, Saskatoon, Saskatchewan, Canada) taught almost every subject including major academic subjects, special education, physical education, and art at the elementary and junior high levels during his teaching career. Mr. Watson recently retired after 28 years of service in the classroom and now dedicates his time to writing and to the building of a 1934 Ford street rod.

Mr. Watson is the author of *Teacher Smart: 125 Tested Techniques for Classroom Management and Control* and *The Classroom Discipline Problem Solver*, both published by The Center for Applied Research in Education.

Mr. Watson also conducts in-service programs for teachers, parent–teacher associations, and health organizations. Mr. Watson has also authored several short stories for magazines and a book on street rodding skills. He can be contacted at geobravo396@hotmail.com.

About the Hooked on Learning Library

The *Hooked on Learning Library* is a comprehensive, three-book series featuring teacher- and student-friendly activity sheets for the secondary classroom in the areas of English, Mathematics, and Science.

In writing these books, special effort was taken to understand students from a social, emotional, and cultural perspective. The results of that initiative is that the books are filled with highly-charged, attention-grabbing, and relevant activity sheets that not only cover the content, but also are fun to do.

An excellent educational resource, this series can be used to provide immediate skill reinforcement and to address skill attainment problems, or it can be used as an integral part of the long-term planning of English, Mathematics, and Science programs. *Hooked on Learning* not only fulfills the needs of the "at-risk" student, but it also satisfies the needs of the strong, independent, self-reliant learner.

The three books in the *Hooked on Learning Library* are:

- 190 Ready-to-Use Activities That Make English Fun!
- 190 Ready-to-Use Activities That Make Math Fun!
- 190 Ready-to-Use Activities That Make Science Fun!

All three books in the *Hooked on Learning Library* have unique areas called Quick Access Information pages. These pages target important information and skills to be learned or reinforced prior to commencing the worksheets. The Quick Access Information data may be on a full page or may be presented at the top of the related worksheet. We include flags to indicate the location of the Quick Access Information sites.

QUICK ACCESS
information

ABOUT THIS BOOK

Teachers cannot succeed in the secondary classroom without user-friendly, efficient, and supportive tools that target skill areas needed in today's fast-paced culture. Those tools must hook into existing English skill programs to reinforce learning. Everywhere there are demands on the teacher's time and materials. This English resource and indeed the whole "Hooked on Learning" series has been designed to help ease these stressors in the teacher's life.

190 Ready-to-Use Activities that Make English Fun! presents fundamental English skills that are the backbone of English language instruction. It does this while making learning fun. Many of the worksheets are presented in story formats that have a degree of familiarity for the students.

Throughout this work you will see strategically located "Quick Access Information" flags in the margins. They point to easily understood areas of English instruction that relate to the concept on the page at hand. There are several "Quick Access Information" full pages that have related worksheets following them. These were developed to make the learning of English as successful as possible. You will find them to be a magnificent tool.

This resource of 190 ready-to-use worksheets can be used across the spectrum of English language education from fulfilling the needs of the at-risk student to satisfying the independent requirements of the academically strong achievers. Here are descriptions of the sections you'll find in this book:

- *Section 1, Assertive Vocabulary Development,* leads the way in presenting English vocabulary skills that are student and teacher friendly. "Boxed Vocabulary Creation" is a fine example of this, whereby vocabulary development is presented in a high-interest, puzzle format. Neither students nor teachers have to wade through a mountain of text in order to grasp the English concepts.

- *Section 2, Grammar in the Communication Process,* identifies very important grammar skills that are so necessary in our modern society. In "Adverbs for Akira and Sonia," for example, students learn the meaning and functional use of adverbs as they are presented in a humorous and recognizable story.

- *Section 3, English Concepts and Techniques to Stimulate and Enrich,* goes beyond grammar to look at how the techniques of the English language work in everyday life. "Learning about Syllables" is great for this. Here understanding of syllables is taught through a story that involves Bighampton Butler Jones in a captivating situation written to appeal to today's students.

- *Section 4, Essential Strategies for Language Development,* looks in depth at those necessary strategies and processes for proper English expression. The activity "Lazy Language Puzzle" has hooked into these concepts nicely. It shows how certain expressions and weak speech habits, while being common in everyday life, are not the correct form of English for success.

- *Section 5, Thinking and Reasoning Skill Builders,* hooks those English concepts that require intellectual understanding to logical deductive reasoning skills. "Following Directions" is a prime example. While the page looks easy, it takes ability in order to succeed by following the pattern. This intellectual challenge will cause students to concentrate and be attentive to the task.

- *Section 6, Problem Solving to Improve Word Use and Understanding,* motivates students to strengthen their personal language skills. "Word Completions: Parts One and Two" are good exercises in this area, wherein students, through an unusual format, are called upon to develop the correct responses.

- *Section 7, Hooked on Creative Writing and Visual Expression,* inspires students to combine visual skills with creative writing. "I Say the Earth Is Flat" is a wonderful illustration of this. Students are not only required to explain their view of flat Earth but are asked to draw and therefore visualize their concept of this idea.

This resource was intensely researched and many hours were spent not only by myself but also by the excellent experienced teacher and student advisors, wonderful stenographer, and professional illustrator who worked to enhance its contents.

Having worked in school systems for 28 years, I know and have experienced the varied workload and broad spectrum of learning needs in all classrooms. I want you to "hook" into this experience. Good luck!

George Watson

CONTENTS

Section 2
GRAMMAR IN THE COMMUNICATION PROCESS   33

Section 3
ENGLISH CONCEPTS AND TECHNIQUES TO STIMULATE AND ENRICH   77

Section 4
ESSENTIAL STRATEGIES FOR LANGUAGE DEVELOPMENT   99

Section 5
THINKING AND REASONING SKILL BUILDERS   125

Section 6
PROBLEM SOLVING TO IMPROVE WORD USE AND UNDERSTANDING   149

Section 7
HOOKED ON CREATIVE WRITING AND VISUAL EXPRESSION   177

SECTION 1

ASSERTIVE VOCABULARY DEVELOPMENT

1. Developing Vocabulary: Part One

★ **Choose the word or phrase in each line that gives the best meaning of the word in bold print.**

1. **large** ➜ big, heavy, tough _____

2. **colossal** ➜ horrible, hairy, huge _____

3. **fear** ➜ chicken, worry, suspicion _____

4. **operate** ➜ die, manage, cut meat _____

5. **noun** ➜ frown; a person, place, or thing; clown _____

6. **good** ➜ virtue, hate, video games _____

7. **focus** ➜ try, concentrate, eat _____

8. **fluid** ➜ solid, liquid, gas _____

9. **evict** ➜ remove, event, evade _____

10. **envy** ➜ empty, desire, evade _____

11. **attire** ➜ black rubber circle, holds air on a car, dress _____

12. **gravity** ➜ up, down, weight _____

13. **grope** ➜ fumble, horse, drugs _____

14. **gruesome** ➜ aging, getting taller, ghastly _____

15. **chronic** ➜ crying, persistent, a sad baby _____

16. **caustic** ➜ corrosive, to cause events, casualty _____

17. **bless** ➜ a Chinese meal, glorify, rest _____

18. **bluster** ➜ boasting, pig, storm _____

19. **crouch** ➜ a place to sit, bend, feel pain _____

20. **luminous** ➜ glowing, a rug-making machine, elephant _____

3

2. Developing Vocabulary: Part Two

★ Describe how the words in each pair are different or similar in meaning. A dictionary will help. *Example:* go, come—The word "go" means to leave here for another place. The word "come" means to leave another place to arrive here.

1. forward, backward _____
_____

2. money, debt _____
_____

3. pirate, captain _____
_____

4. dream, nightmare _____
_____

5. video, baseball _____
_____

6. monkey, baboon _____
_____

7. magnet, gravity _____
_____

8. spinster, bachelor _____
_____

9. menu, truck _____
_____

10. tomato, mango _____
_____

11. street car, subway _____
_____

12. fear, joy _____
_____

Name_____ Date _____

3. Solving Word Problems: Part One

★ Rearrange the letters in each box to form three words.

★ The last or longest word is a synonym of the word "happiness" (all letters must be used).

★ The two middle words do not need to be a synonym of the word "happiness." These two middle words can be shorter words using some of the letters in the box on the left.

Each word in the column below is a synonym of *happiness.*

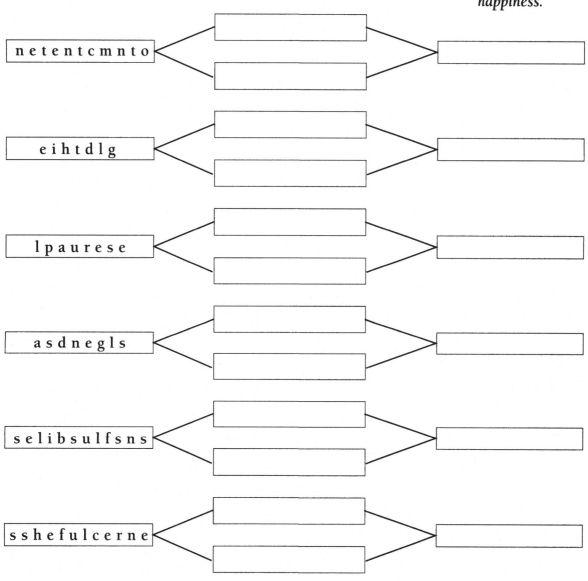

n e t e n t c m n t o

e i h t d l g

l p a u r e s e

a s d n e g l s

s e l i b s u l f s n s

s s h e f u l c e r n e

5

4. Solving Word Problems: Part Two

★   Rearrange the letters in each rectangle to form three words.

★   The last or longest word is a synonym of the word "awesome" (all letters must be used).

★   The two middle words do not need to be a synonym of the word "awesome." These two middle words can be shorter words using some of the letters in the box on the left.

Each word is a synonym of *awesome*.

c i a s t t f n a

l o d r f e n w u

u e b r p s

r e o s u l v a m

t a n o g u s t d i n

b l u s o f a u

Name_____ Date _____

5. Letter Replacements

★ Use the letters in the word above each column to complete the chart. E... word contains each letter at least once. The letters are not always in th... they appear in the word above each column. All the words needed for b... columns are in the Choice Box below.

Use letters in EAT	Use letters in TIE
1. b __ __ __	13. __ __ __ n a g __ r
2. n __ __ __	14. __ __ d __
3. a s s i s __ __ n c __	15. __ __ n s __ l
4. r __ __ __	16. b __ s __ c __
5. d __ m o n s __ r __ t __	17. __ __ __-d y __
6. d i s __ __ n c __	18. a d j __ c __ __ v __
7. s __ f __ __ y	19. __ __ g __ r
8. s __ l u __ __	20. m __ n __ __ __ o n
9. __ __ __ c h __ r	21. __ l __ c __ r __ c
10. __ __ v __ r n	22. __ n d __ c __ n __
11. __ __ s __ __ l __ s s	23. g __ n __ r o s __ __ y
12. i m p o r __ __ n c __	24. __ n v __ __ __

Choice Box

adjective	electric	neat	teache...
assistance	generosity	rate	teenag...
beat	importance	safety	tide
bisect	indecent	salute	tie-dye...
demonstrate	invite	tasteless	tiger
distance	mention	tavern	tinsel

6. Video-Game Consonant Search

★ All the consonants have been removed in the puzzle below. Using words from the Choice Box, fill in the missing consonants.

★ All the words have been taken from common video games.

1. E __ E __ __ __ O __ I __

2. __ __ A __

3. O __ __ I __ E

4. I __ __ A __ E __

5. __ __ __ I __ __

6. A __ I E __

7. A __ __ E __ __ U __ E

8. __ O __ E __

9. __ A __ U __ __ __

10. __ O __ U E

11. O __ __ O __ E __ __

12. __ E __ A

13. __ O __ __

14. __ __ A __ O

15. __ E A __

16. E __ __ __ E __ E

17. __ __ I __ E __

18. __ A __ I __ __

19. A __ __ I O __

20. __ E __ A __

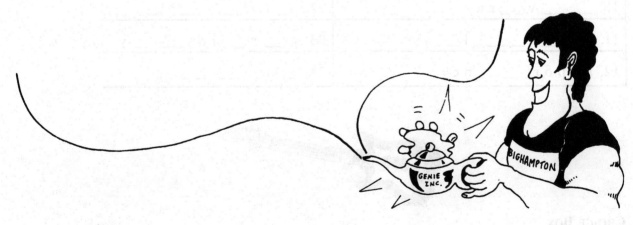

CHOICE BOX

ACTION	EXTREME	MEGA	ROGUE
ADVENTURE	GAMING	METAL	SHIVER
ALIEN	HEAT	ONLINE	STAR
DRAGON	INVADER	OPPONENT	THRILL
ELECTRONIC	LAUNCH	POWER	WORM

Name_____ Date _____

7. Word Builder with Letter "W"

★ Choose a set of letters from the Choice Box to complete the words in the alphabetical list. Some sets of letters are used more than once. Some sets are not used at all.

1.		A	th		14.		N	ess
2.		B	ehaved		15.		O	ck
3.		C	h		16.		P	ed
4.		D	cat		17.		Q	uest
5.		E	ther		18.		R	oom
6.		F	e		19.		S	t
7.		G	ht		20.		T	ap
8.		H	in		21.		U	p
9.		I	sker		22.		V	er
10.		J	ammer		23.		W	eek
11.		K	ing		24.		X	en
12.		L	nut		25.		Y	ward
13.		M	up		26.		Z	ard

CHOICE BOX

wa	warp	well	wind	woo
waf	wash	wh	wire	work
wai	web	whate	wish	wort
wal	wedl	wi	wit	wr
war	wei	wil	wo	wren
ward				

8. Ice Hockey Vocabulary

★ Each sport has its own set of words or vocabulary. Your task is to use the Choice Box to find the correct hockey word to suit the description.

1. A round, black, rubber disc that is shot into the goal: _____
2. Name of the person attending the goal: _____
3. Color of the line in the middle of the ice surface: _____
4. Name of the people watching the game: _____
5. Name of the duration of each game segment: _____
6. Person behind the players' bench directing the players: _____
7. Name of the NHL trophy: _____
8. Name of the Boston team: _____
9. Padded devices worn on the players' hands: _____
10. Plastic object worn on the head of each player: _____
11. The bottom of a player's stick is wrapped with this: _____
12. Where the person sits to identify whether or not a goal is scored: _____
13. Worn on the players' feet: _____
14. Worn on the legs to prevent injury from hard shots: _____
15. Where offending players are placed for penalties: _____
16. Name of the building games are played in: _____
17. What players must do to get ready for games: _____
18. Letter on front of Boston team jerseys: _____
19. Number of players on the ice at one time for each team: _____
20. Worn by goalie for leg protection: _____
21. Worn by goalie for upper body protection: _____
22. Worn by all players for neck and shoulder protection: _____
23. These separate the players from the audience: _____
24. Length of time for a minor penalty: _____
25. Device used by the players to shoot the puck: _____

CHOICE BOX

arena	chest pads	goalie pads	practice	skates
B	coach	helmet	puck	Stanley Cup
boards	fans	knee & shin pads	red	stick
Bruins	gloves	penalty box	shoulder pads	tape
cage	goalie	period	six	two minutes

Name_____ Date _____

9. Pick a Sport: Part One

★ **Discover the sport from the description of its equipment or action. Find your answers in the Choice Box below.**

1. A circular sphere whose covering is made of leather that can often be thrown so that it curves sideways: _____

2. A white ball that is often "spiked" as players jump near a net: _____

3. A long spear-like device whose distance thrown is measured: _____

4. Usually a white ball with dimples: _____

5. A brown ball pointed at both ends that is often punted: _____

6. The picking up of heavy, disk-like objects at the ends of bars: _____

7. A bouncy little white ball about the size of a golf ball that isn't a golf ball:

   _____

8. The jumping out of a heavier-than-air machine at several thousand feet of altitude hoping one's parachute was correctly packed: _____

9. Pointy shafts propelled towards targets: _____

10. The going up and coming down from large metamorphic objects:

    _____

HE'S SO CUTE WITH THOSE DIMPLES.

CHOICE BOX

archery	mountain climbing
baseball	skydiving
football	table tennis
golf	vollyball
javelin	weightlifting

10. Pick a Sport: Part Two

★ Here are some more sports-related words to enrich your vocabulary.

★ Discover the sport from the description of its equipment or action. Find your answers in the Choice Box below.

1. Two flat boards curved at the forward tips worn on the feet for sliding in the snow:

   _____

2. A round ball about 10 to 12 inches in diameter with finger holes in it:

   _____

3. A black hard rubber device that is usually frozen before playing a professional game of this: _____

4. A round saucer-shaped device thrown with one hand: _____

5. A spherical metal ball projected from the hand as the hand is bent to the shoulder area: _____

6. A hanging net through which a ball is slam dunked: _____

7. Water: _____

8. A device sometimes with feathers on it and cone-shaped: _____

9. Fighting with a foil, saber, or epee; often seen in 16th-century adventure movies:

   _____

10. An oval-shaped bat with webbing; sometimes the score is called "love":

    _____

CHOICE BOX

badminton	hockey
basketball	shot put
bowling	skiing
discus	swimming
fencing (sword fighting)	tennis

Copyright © 2002 by John Wiley & Sons, Inc.

11. Grouping Sports Vocabulary

★   Choose words or expressions from the Choice Box that fit each sport.

★   Cross off the words after you use them.

★   No word can be used more than once.

★   Some words may not be used at all.

SPORT	WORDS
1. Basketball	
2. Ice Hockey	
3. Tennis	
4. Baseball	
5. Football	
6. Cycling	
7. Skiing	
8. Volleyball	
9. Golf	
10. Skydiving	
11. Car Racing	
12. Arm Wrestling	
13. Boat Racing	
14. Bowling	
15. Archery	

CHOICE BOX

wheel, puck, bow, engine, green, upper body strength, parachute, skate, Tour de France, arrow, field goal, gutter, out, pins, net, pedals, alley, blade, slam dunk, strike, Celtics, slider, tee, hull, propeller, putter, center, floor, shoot, racket, helmet, spike, bail, left wing, mogul, pitch, poles, set, target, anchor, homer, love, wax, fifteen, 50-yard line, serve, touchdown, pigskin, gravity, ripcord, grip, muscles, wrist, power

12. Sports Spelling

★ Each partially spelled word, phrase, or term below has something to do with sports. Your task is to complete the word using the sport as a clue. A Choice Box has been provided.

1. t __ __ c h __ __ __ n
   football

2. __ __ __ e __ __ __ __
   baseball

3. __ __ l __ - __ n - __ __ __
   golf

4. __ __ c q u e t
   tennis

5. __ l __ m __ u __ __
   basketball

6. __ __ o s s __ __ __ __ k
   ice hockey

7. __ __ r __ t __ __ n
   running

8. __ __ __ e __ __ __ l __
   swimming

9. __ __ __ __ d
   diving

10. I __ __ i __ n __ p __ l __ __ 50 __
    car racing

11. f __ e __ __ __   __ o __ l
    football

12. t __ __ ro __ __ h __ r __ __
    horse racing

13. __ __ t t __ r __ __ y
    swimming

14. __ __ __ __ e __
    basketball

15. l __ __ __
    fishing

16. __ __ n __ h   p __ e __ __
    weightlifting

17. __ a r __ __ h __ __ e
    skydiving

18. __ a __ g   __ __ __ __
    surfing

19. __ __ __ u l
    skiing

20. __ __ i __ __ l __
    basketball

21. __ __ n a
    fishing

22. __ k __ t __ s
    ice hockey

23. t h __ __ __   __ a __ __
    baseball

24. __ __ e   o __ __
    golf

25. e n __ __ __ __ __
    motor racing

CHOICE BOX

bench press	engine	homerun	parachute	third base
board	field goal	Indianapolis 500	racquet	thoroughbred
butterfly	freestyle	lure	skates	touchdown
crosscheck	hang ten	marathon	slam dunk	travel
dribble	hole-in-one	mogul	tee off	tuna

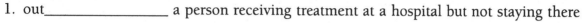

13. The Great Search for "Out" Words

★ **Find compound words that fit these definitions.**

★ **All words begin with the word "out."**

1. out_____ a person receiving treatment at a hospital but not staying there

2. out_____ an old-fashioned thing; something not in present use

3. out_____ something not inside

4. out_____ a way of thinking about things or an attitude of the mind

5. out_____ the amount produced in a factory or by a student

6. out_____ a very angry feeling

7. out_____ means to ride faster than other

8. out_____ to reach beyond

9. out_____ means to run faster than others

10. out_____ to shine brighter than another

11. out_____ means to talk more than others

12 out_____ to defeat in voting

13. out_____ to shoot better than anyone else

14. out_____ means to be at the start of something

15. out_____ in the military, one person is higher in command than another

16. out_____ a larger-than-usual size

17. out_____ to score more than others

18. out_____ the farthest out

19. out_____ to be very frank and not hold back what you want to say

20. out_____ to be more clever than your opponent

14. Boxed Vocabulary Creation

★ Use this box of letters to form new words from the letters that are next to each other.

★ The letters to make the words may be used up or down, right or left, or diagonal from each other. The first one is done for you to help you get started.

★ Each word has a free "starting" letter in the working list below.

C	O	R	E
P	C	A	M
I	K	G	E
T	E	Y	A

WORKING LIST

1. C <u>R</u> <u>E</u> <u>A</u> <u>M</u>

2. O ___

3. C ___ ___

4. G ___ ___

5. C ___ ___ ___

6. G ___ ___ ___

7. A ___ ___

8. S ___ ___ ___ ___

9. P ___ ___ ___ ___

10. S ___ ___ ___ ___

11. G ___ ___

12. M ___ ___ ___

13. M ___ ___ ___

14. B ___ ___ ___

15. B ___ ___ ___

16. B ___ ___ ___ ___

17. B ___ ___

18. S ___ ___ ___

19. S ___ ___ ___

20. S ___ ___ ___

15. Workers' Vocabulary Puzzle: Part One

★ Use the clues from the sentences to fill in the missing letters on the puzzle. The word you need is scrambled after each sentence.

1. People who grow crops and raise cattle are called _____. AMRERFS

2. A worker's lunch must be well packed so it doesn't _____. POLIS

3. After working hard each day, you will be _____. REITD

4. The bank is a good place to _____ your money. EOSIDPT

5. In India many people work with _____ which are sometimes called pachyderms. NATSHPLEE

6. When you go home from your job, you _____ work. EVEAL

7. _____ are flown by a pilot and co-pilot. ERLAAIPNS

8. Car radiators are _____ in a mechanic's shop. PRDEAREI

9. If someone tells you where a good job is, this is really great _____. TANOIFIRMON

10. _____ of ideas and equipment help other workers. ARHINGS

11. Orchard workers pick _____ from trees. UTIRF

12. _____ of outside workers must be covered in winter. SDAHN

1.	F			M			
2.		P			L		
3.					D		
4.		E		O		T	
5.			E	P			T	S
6.			A				
7.		I	R	P			
8.	R					D	
9.		N			R		O	
10.		H		R			
11.			U				
12.			N				

OPPORTUNITY

16. Workers' Vocabulary Puzzle: Part Two

★ Use the clues from the sentences to fill in the missing letters on the puzzle. The word you need is scrambled after each sentence.

1. _____ envelopes are given to employees on payday. AYP

2. _____ workers do not last long on the job. AYZL

3. Goggles can provide _____ protection at work. YEE

4. _____ are required to mail letters to employers. NVLPSOEEE

5. _____ workers are a source of good advice. LERDO

6. _____ with disabilities make excellent employees. EPELOP

7. _____ can be earned from a job. OYNME

8. _____ at work on time is important. RRAIVGNI

9. Some scissors are made for _____-handed people. ETLF

10. _____ shoelaces properly is a job-safety requirement. YNGIT

11. When some people are _____, they still like to work even though they don't need the money. HRIC

12. Everyone should _____ breakfast because it is the most important meal of the day. TAE

Copyright © 2002 by John Wiley & Sons, Inc.

Name_____ Date _____

17. Work-World Vocabulary: Part One

★ Rewrite each sentence below by replacing the underlined phrase with a word from the Choice Box.

1. On the job today workers must be able to <u>talk and relay information to each other</u>.

   _____

   _____

2. When preparing food at a restaurant, a chef heats the ingredients on a <u>hot, dark surface with a flame or electric current running through it</u>. _____

   _____

3. A dentist must have good wrist technique to pull <u>those white, hard, chewing devices from a person's mouth</u>. _____

   _____

4. In the future, many more jobs will require you to know how to use <u>electronic devices with a screen and a keyboard</u>. _____

   _____

5. A cobbler is a person who works with <u>coverings people wear on the lowest part of the human body</u>. _____

   _____

6. In today's and tomorrow's work world, students will need to adapt to <u>their world being in a constant state of being different</u>. _____

   _____

7. A good work communication skill is being able to <u>hear what other people are saying</u>.

   _____

   _____

CHOICE BOX

change	listen	stove
communicate	shoes	teeth
computers		

Name_____ Date _____

18. Work-World Vocabulary: Part Two

★ **Rewrite each sentence below by replacing the underlined phrase with a word from the Choice Box.**

1. Getting into a <u>verbal or physical hassle</u> with your fellow workers is not very productive.

   _____

   _____

2. The employer expects you to not <u>take products, tools, or other materials home without permission.</u> _____

   _____

3. Have you ever seen <u>people who wear blue uniforms and control crime</u> make an arrest?

   _____

   _____

4. The <u>person in charge and who has responsibility</u> usually has the last say when making decisions on the job. _____

   _____

5. It must be fun to work at <u>those places where there are Ferris wheels, bumper cars, and roller coasters.</u> _____

   _____

6. If I were in a factory, I would like to run one of those <u>machines that work almost by themselves and seem to have electronic brains.</u> _____

   _____

7. Workers using power tools should wear <u>coverings usually made of tough plastic</u> to protect their eyes. _____

   _____

CHOICE BOX		
face shields	police officers	state fairs
fight	robots	steal
manager		

19. Employment Vocabulary

★ Twelve important jobs are listed on the left. Write on the line two words related to each job. Then, on another sheet of paper, use those two words in a proper sentence to describe that job.

1. Nurse

_____

2. Teacher

_____

3. Truck Driver

_____

4. Pilot

_____

5. Soldier

_____

6. Entertainer

_____

7. Coach

_____

8. Religious Leader

_____

9. Radio Announcer

_____

10. Electrician

_____

11. Plumber

_____

12. Firefighter

_____

20. Choosing Work-Related Vocabulary: Part One

★ Read the following sentences and replace the underlined word or phrase with the most suitable work-related word you can find in the Choice Box below.

1. Medical people who perform surgery must wear special clothing that is sterile.

   _____

2. Many offices have days when workers can wear nonformal clothing.

   _____

3. On Halloween, even office workers will sometimes wear strange and unusual attire.

   _____

4. When some people work with very noisy machines, they must wear devices that deaden the sound in their ears. _____

5. A person who does deep sea diving must wear rubber extensions on his or her feet to aid swimming. _____

6. A soldier must polish the fasteners on his or her uniform for inspection by officers.

   _____

7. Many people who secretly discover who has committed a crime do not wear a police uniform. _____

8. Dock workers must often wear protective leather coverings for their hands as they handle ships' cargoes. _____

9. Strings that keep shoes together must be tied properly as a safety feature on many jobs. _____

10. People who ride horses in races must be highly skilled. _____

Copyright © 2002 by John Wiley & Sons, Inc.

CHOICE BOX

buttons	costumes	detectives	ear plugs
flippers	gloves	informal	jockeys
laces	surgeons		

Name_____ Date _____

21. Choosing Work-Related Vocabulary: Part Two

★ **Read the following sentences and replace the underlined phrase with the most suitable work-related word you can find in the Choice Box below.**

1. Construction-site workers must wear <u>hard protective or metal coverings for the head</u>. _____

2. Many workers in industry must wear <u>steel-toed leather coverings for their feet</u>. _____

3. It may be dangerous for a person to wear <u>long dangling jewelry from their ears</u> when working around moving machines. _____

4. A dentist must wear <u>latex coverings</u> on his or her hands when working in a person's mouth. _____

5. Outside construction workers must wear <u>thick padded coverings for the arms and bodies</u> in order to keep warm in winter. _____

6. Working on cars will get clothing covered with <u>a black greasy substance from the motor</u> that is often hard to wash out. _____

7. Have you ever seen the <u>persons who control crime</u> make an arrest? _____

8. People using power tools should wear <u>coverings usually made of tough see-through plastic</u> to protect their eyes. _____

9. It is important for some workers to wear a <u>time-keeping device</u> on their wrist. _____

10. Sometimes a <u>black circular rubber part on a car</u> will go flat and a person must change it. _____

CHOICE BOX

earrings	oil	rubber gloves	watch
face shields	parkas	tire	work boots
hard hats	police		

22. Positive Vocabulary Puzzle

★ Your task is to choose positive words from the Choice Box to help you complete
the spelling of the words in the puzzle.

CHOICE BOX

blessing, excellent, fabulous, fantastic, favor, gain, good, great, happiness, joy, love,
marvelous, merit, positive, powerful, prize, profit, right, spectacular, splendid, striking,
stupendous, success, superb, terrific

Name_____ Date _____

23. Word Builder–Deceptive Words

★ Listed below are 12 words that are related to the word "deception." Your task on *line a* is to write down what you think the word means. On *line b*, write the dictionary definition of the word.

1. deceit   (a) _____

        (b) _____

2. fraud   (a) _____

        (b) _____

3. duplicity   (a) _____

        (b) _____

4. bluff   (a) _____

        (b) _____

5. cunning   (a) _____

        (b) _____

6. treachery   (a) _____

        (b) _____

7. beguilement   (a) _____

        (b) _____

8. chicanery   (a) _____

        (b) _____

9. skulduggery   (a) _____

        (b) _____

10. rogue   (a) _____

        (b) _____

11. shenanigans   (a) _____

        (b) _____

12. hypocrisy   (a) _____

        (b) _____

24. Word Builder—Exciting Words

★ Listed below are 12 words that are related to the word "excitement." Your task on *line a* is to write down what you think the word means. On *line b*, write the dictionary definition of the word.

1. hoopla   (a) _____

    (b) _____

2. thrill   (a) _____

    (b) _____

3. titillation   (a) _____

    (b) _____

4. effervescence   (a) _____

    (b) _____

5. frenzy   (a) _____

    (b) _____

6. hysterical   (a) _____

    (b) _____

7. electrify   (a) _____

    (b) _____

8. glamorize   (a) _____

    (b) _____

9. ebullient   (a) _____

    (b) _____

10. liveliness   (a) _____

    (b) _____

11. stimulating   (a) _____

    (b) _____

12. sensational   (a) _____

    (b) _____

Name_____ Date _____

25. Rich Word Puzzle

★ Some words in the English language have a genuine richness to their use, sound, and meaning.

★ Take the words from the Choice Box below and place them in the puzzle where they fit. The vowels (A, E, I, O, U) have been inserted.

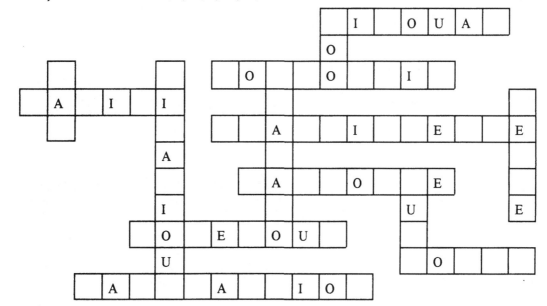

CHOICE BOX

bivouac	frankincense	horsy	wapiti
boo	gargoyle	lush	yaw
bravado	genre	rapscallion	
covetous	hobgoblin	vivacious	

26. The Wright Brothers and Spelling

★ Words associated with the Wright Brothers are shown with all the vowels in the correct positions. All you need to do is fill in the consonants. Cross off each consonant as it is used. There is a Choice Box below.

★ Answer the "Extra Credit" question at the bottom of the page.

B B B   C C C C C   D D   F F F   G G G G   H H H H   K K K
L L L L L L L L L L   M   N N N N N N N N   P P P   R R R R R R R R R
S S S S S   T T T T T T T   V V V   W W W W

1. _ _ I _ _ _

2. A I _ _ _ _ A _ E

3. O _ _ I _ _ E

4. _ I _ E

5. _ _ I _ E _

6. _ I _ Y _ _ E

7. A I _

8. _ I _ _ Y _ A _ _

9. _ A _ _ _ E _ _

10. _ I _ _

11. _ I _ _ U _

12. _ _ Y I _ _

13. _ I _ _

14. _ E _ A I _ _

15. _ I _ O _

16. _ U _ _ E _

17. _ _ O _ _ E _ _

18. _ A _ _ I _ E

19. I _ _ E _ E _ _

20. _ U _ _ E _ _ _ U _

Extra Credit Question: Where is the reflection of the Wright Brothers' plane?

_____

CHOICE BOX

air	flying	machine	tunnel
airplane	glider	Orville	Van Cleve
bicycle	interest	pilot	Wilbur
brothers	kite	repairs	wind
flight	Kitty Hawk	successful	wing

28

27. Auto Vocabulary

★ Read the sentences and find the missing words in the Choice Box.

★ Write your answer for each sentence on the puzzle.

★ When completed, the boxes will spell the names of two different totally awesome cars.

___(1)___ can be fun if the car runs well.

Many people go to car ___(2)___ at a track.

___(3)___ is often used as fuel in race cars. You should not drive if you drink it.

___(4)___ is the main fuel in automobiles.

Race tracks are sometimes called ___(5)___ .

___(6)___ are black, round, and made of rubber.

Your ___(7)___ time is how long it took you to run in a drag race.

___(8)___ gear is not as important as the forward gear in a race car.

___(9)___ used to pull buggies in the old days.

___(10)___ cars are now being restored.

The ___(11)___ in a car delivers power from the motor to the rear wheels.

At the back of a car are the ___(12)___ wheels.

Many race tracks are in the shape of an ___(13)___ .

___(14)___ of cars must always keep safety in mind.

1. ☐ _ _ _ _ _ _ _

2. ☐ _ _ _ _ _

3. ☐ _ _ _ _ _ _ _

4. ☐ _ _ _

5. ☐ _ _ _ _ _ _ _ _

6. ☐ _ _ _ _ _

7. ☐ _ _ _ _ _ _ _

8. ☐ _ _ _ _ _ _ _

9. ☐ _ _ _ _ _ _

10. ☐ _ _ _

11. ☐ _ _ _ _ _ _ _ _ _ _ _ _

12. ☐ _ _ _ _

13. ☐ _ _ _ _

14. ☐ _ _ _ _ _ _ _

CHOICE BOX

alcohol	elapsed	old	rear	tires
drivers	gas	oval	reverse	transmission
driving	horses	races	speedways	

Name _____ Date _____

28. Hot-Rod Vocabulary Every Teenager Should Know

★ Fill in the blanks with the correct words or expressions from the Choice Box.

1. The 426 Chrysler Hemi Motor is nicknamed _____.

2. After market tubes on the side of a motor through which exhaust flows are called _____.

3. Magnesium or chrome wheels are called _____.

4. This is the name given to a hot rod made from a 1923 Model T open car body. _____

5. The amount of lugging power of a motor is called _____.

6. The _____ is called the "true" American sports car.

7. If you put a huge motor in a smaller car, you often need a hood _____ in order to close the hood.

8. A four-cylinder motor is usually not as powerful as a _____.

9. At a car race, the _____ _____ prepares the race care for action.

10. The nickname for a 1932 Ford coupe made into a hot rod is _____.

11. The _____ was the first pony car of the 1960s.

12. The Bonneville _____ _____ in the state of _____ are used to set speed records.

13. Hot rods are also called _____.

14. When Joe squealed the tires, they said he _____.

15. Power in a motor is measured in _____.

CHOICE BOX

King Kong, 23T Bucket, mags, Corvette, Deuce Coupe, horsepower, pit crew, V8, scoop, Mustang, Utah, headers, torque, street rods, burned rubber, Salt Flats

29. Auto Vocabulary for a Mobile Society

★　Write the word from the Choice Box that best suits each car function.

1. _____: a hinged cover for the motor
2. _____: wheels made of magnesium, sometimes chrome plated
3. _____: covers the inside of the door and has the inside door handle on it
4. _____: mixes the fuel with the air on top of the motor
5. _____: you store things in here for security
6. _____: these need to be buckled up
7. _____: you put a key in this to start the car
8. _____: you push this to make a noise
9. _____: a decoration on top of the hood
10. _____: used at night so the driver can see the road
11. _____: distributes electrical impulses to the spark plugs in the motor
12. _____: covers the ceiling or inside roof of a car
13. _____: holds the front wheels onto the axle
14. _____: device blows up to protect you when your car is hit from the front
15. _____: the glass directly in front of the driver
16. _____: wires are routed all over the car through this
17. _____: the noise of the car is lessened by exhaust traveling through this
18. _____: have faces and tell you how well the car is operating
19. _____: device transfers power from the motor to the driving wheels
20. _____: device is on top of the motor and filters the air
21. _____: has fans and cools the water or antifreeze
22. _____: the whole car is powered by this machine
23. _____: circular discs that cover the wheels
24. _____: at the front of the car and is bolted to the body
25. _____: the metal skin of the car

CHOICE BOX

carburetor, air cleaner, transmission, radiator, motor, grill, body, gauges, muffler, hub-caps, spindle, mag wheels, hood, trunk, hood ornament, seat belts, headlights, air bag, windshield, door panel, head liner, distributor, wiring harness, ignition switch, horn button

Name_____ Date _____

30. Plymouth Colony Reinforcers

★ Hidden in each diagram is one Plymouth Colony related word. Draw a continuous line through the letters as you spell each word correctly. The letters are not in a straight line. Each word has 7 letters.

A	P	C	O	M
T	D	E	W	P
T	Q	B	I	A
A	U	T	T	C
L	O	L	V	J

A	M	R	W	V
X	P	U	E	I
U	I	R	O	T
V	T	E	B	K
S	A	N	Y	M

P	J	N	O	P
I	L	U	C	E
G	H	G	T	T
B	C	J	R	N
D	Y	N	I	M

★ Each word has a set of missing double letters. Add the missing letters to complete the words.

HO __ __ A N D   P E R M I __ __ I O N   S L __ __ P I N G

E __ __ E C T   O P P R E __ __ I V E   S P __ __ D W E L L

S E __ __ L E   F R __ __ D O M   F I N A __ __ Y

★ Beside each word is a clue to the word. All the vowels have been filled in.

__ __ I __   (boat)   __ A I __ __   (belief)

__ O Y A __ E   (sea trip)   __ __ E E __ O __ (no restrictions)

__ A Y __ __ O __ E __ (ship's name)   __ O U __ A __ E (bravery)

SECTION 2

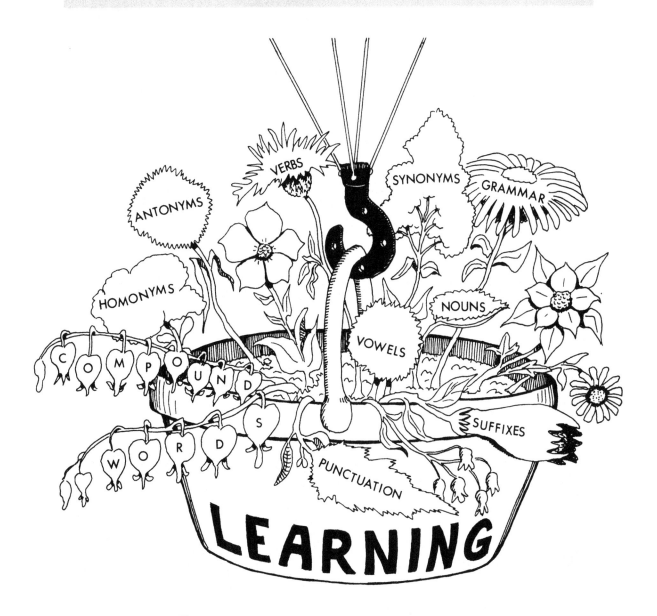

GRAMMAR IN THE COMMUNICATION PROCESS

Name_____ Date _____

31. Important Definitions Made Easy

Noun: The name of a person, place, or thing.

teacher park horse

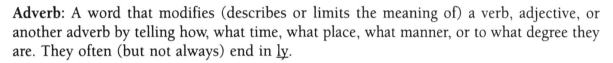

QUICK ACCESS
information

Verb: An action word.

jump

Pronoun: A word that takes the place of a noun.

Connie ate supper. She ate supper.

Adverb: A word that modifies (describes or limits the meaning of) a verb, adjective, or another adverb by telling how, what time, what place, what manner, or to what degree they are. They often (but not always) end in ly.

He spoke loudly.

Adjective: A word that modifies (describes or limits the meaning of) a noun.

the green dress

Synonym: A word that has the same or almost the same meaning as another word. The two words have different spellings and sounds.

happy and joyous

Homonym: A word that sounds the same as another word but the meaning is different and the spelling is usually different.

bear and bare

Antonym: A word that means the opposite of another word. They are sometimes called "word opposites."

go and come

Homograph: A word that is spelled the same as another but with a different meaning and, sometimes, a different pronunciation.

bow (front part of ship), bow (to bend), bow (a decorative knot)

Name_____ Date_____

32. Identifying English Grammar

★ Shown below is a grid with different English grammar terms above a set of lines. You are to choose suitable words from the Choice Box to fit into each category.

★ Each word you choose must begin with the letter to the left.

	NOUNS	VERBS	ADVERBS	ADJECTIVES
E				
N				
G				
L				
I				
S				
H				

CHOICE BOX

elegant	grow	internally	new
elephant	happily	introduce	newly
evade	hard	lately	Norman
eventually	hat	lettuce	shut
goulash	hum	lift	slowly
greatly	India	little	solid
green	inner	navigate	sugar

33. Common and Proper Nouns: Part One

QUICK ACCESS information

Quick Access Information ➜ A common noun is the name of any person, place, or thing, e.g., *pencil*. A proper noun is the name of a particular person, place, or thing and begins with a capital letter, e.g., *Bighampton Butler Jones*.

★ Choose only the proper nouns from the list to complete the puzzle. The boxed letters will reveal an important truth. Be careful! The proper nouns must be capitalized.

1. | | o __ __ y   spokane
2. | | m __ __ a   tiger   oregon
3. | | __ __ s __   tommy
4. | | __ v __ r __   yuma   savanna
5. | | __ __ o r __ __ __   canada
6. | | __ __ a h __ __ __   school
7. | | r __ __ __ n   boise
8. | | i __ __ __ __ n   orlando   elephant
9. | | c __ __ __ __ __ n   spikes   colorado
10. | | __ m __ a   oklahoma   alabama
11. | A | l __ __ __ __ __   buffalo   larado
12. | | __ __ a   scranton   ohio
13. | I | __ __ __   hawaii
14. | N | __ __ __ __ __ k __   suburbs   pinto horse
15. | | __ __ k __ __ e   elvira
16. | | __ n __ __ a   omaha   lincoln
17. | | __ w __ __ i   ten   cows
18. | | h __ __   tampa   afghan hound
19. | | __ __ __ __ d __   nebraska   iowa
20. | | a __ __ d __   seven   state

Name_____ Date _____

34. Common and Proper Nouns: Part Two

Copyright © 2002 by John Wiley & Sons, Inc.

QUICK ACCESS information

Quick Access Information ➔ A common noun is the name of any person, place, or thing, e.g., *lion*. A proper noun is the name of a particular person, place, or thing and begins with a capital letter, e.g., *Jamalia Sousa*.

★ Listed below are 40 words or groups of words. Some are proper nouns requiring capitals and some are common nouns that do not require a capital. Some have capitals in the wrong location.

★ Your task is to rewrite each word using capital letters in their correct locations, if needed.

hot Dog	_____	pittsBurgH	_____
Red rock river	_____	Park avenUe	_____
gattleburg	_____	DogS	_____
virgiNia	_____	WashingTon Irving	_____
benedicT arnolD	_____	TraInS	_____
missouri riVer	_____	lakE	_____
airplane	_____	womaN	_____
lucky Lady	_____	doctor Smith	_____
rubber Boot	_____	peacock	_____
Jason's rubber boot	_____	Sparrow	_____
george WasHington	_____	roosteR	_____
Bay of bengal	_____	great salt Lake	_____
dallas cowboys	_____	julY	_____
missiSSippI river	_____	wednesdaY	_____
asiA	_____	Kathy	_____
river	_____	boise	_____
lady diana	_____	taXes	_____
queen elizabeth	_____	queen	_____
cowbell	_____	serVant	_____
Marybell	_____	Clara Cow	_____

Name_____ Date_____

35. Buckets of Words

Quick Access Information ➜ A noun is the name of a person, place, or thing. A verb is an action word. An adjective describes a noun. An adverb describes a verb.

★ Pick five nouns, verbs, adjectives, and adverbs in the following sentences and place them in the appropriate bucket.

1. The green funny car squealed its tires menacingly.

2. Forcefully the old cow chased the teenager.

3. "Teacher, may I have a snooze in class?" Bighampton asked hopefully.

4. The old blue bug ate the green giant fly slowly.

5. Lovingly, Kathy cared for her tiny baby.

6. Wild horses stampeded quickly into the old schoolyard.

7. "The United States is the best country in the world," Bighampton said proudly.

8. "Teenage boys are intelligent," Bobby said confidently.

9. "Green people eaters usually wear purple polka-dot bikinis," Jamalia said bashfully.

10. Arrogantly Molly bragged that her wild party dress was awesome and cool.

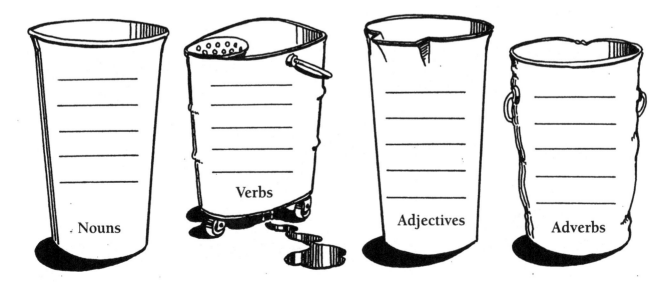

Nouns   Verbs   Adjectives   Adverbs

Name_____ Date_____

36. IDENTIFYING NOUNS, VERBS, AND ADJECTIVES

Quick Access Information → A noun is the name of a person, place, or thing. A verb is an action word. An adjective describes a noun.

★ Read the following sentences and write whether the underlined word is a noun, verb, or adjective.

1. Little Miss Muffet sat on what they now think was a <u>tuffet</u>. _____

2. Little Jack Horner sat in a <u>green</u> corner. _____

3. Mary had a <u>little</u> lamb it is believed. _____

4. Hansel and Gretel <u>met</u> the ugly, but friendly, witch. _____

5. The <u>ugly</u> duckling was emotionally upset. _____

6. The <u>emperor</u> had new clothes, well sort of! _____

7. Peter Pan went to Never <u>Never</u> Land. _____

8. Rapunzel <u>threw</u> down her long hair. _____

9. The Shoemaker and the <u>elves</u> were not heels. _____

10. Little <u>Red</u> Riding Hood feared the wolf. _____

11. The <u>Three</u> Little Pigs ruined the wolf's meal. _____

12. Cinderella had seriously ugly stepsisters. _____

Name _____ Date _____

37. Adjective Power

Quick Access Information → An adjective describes the shape, size, color, etc., of a noun (person, place, or thing). For example, the *small* horse. *Small* is the adjective that describes the size of the horse.

★ Circle the adjectives in the following sentences, Then rewrite the sentence using a different adjective. (NOTE: Some sentences have more than one adjective.) The first one has been done for you.

1. The (old) goose chased Jamalia. _____ **The young goose chased Jamalia.** _____

2. Did that goose lay a golden egg? _____

3. Maybe there are more wonderful, large eggs in her. _____

4. "Let's make delicious goose soup," Bighampton said. _____

5. Jamalia blurted, "Don't hurt the cute goose." _____

6. "Goose meat is good, sweet, and pure," Bighampton retorted. _____

7. Would you hurt a valuable goose that lays golden eggs? _____

8. "Is it real gold," Bighampton queried, "or just Fool's gold?" _____

9. Are the big eggs real, shiny, and heavy? _____

10. What kind of strange goose lays golden, weighty, huge eggs? _____

11. I say let's make a nutritious meal of the less valuable chicken. _____

12. Everyone except the chicken agreed with this brilliant and marvelous idea. _____

38. The Wonderful World of Adjectives and Adverbs

Quick Access Information ➔ Adjectives describe nouns (persons, places, or things). An adverb describes a verb (an action word).

★ **What adjectives describe the following nouns?**

(1) The <u>desk</u> you are sitting at	(2) Your most important <u>friend</u>	(3) Your experiences last <u>weekend</u>
(4) <u>Elephants</u>	(5) Your favorite <u>video game</u>	(6) <u>Cows</u>

★ **What adverbs (often end in "ly") describe each of these verbs?**

(1) How people <u>look</u>	(2) How a video game <u>works</u>	(3) How horses <u>run</u>
(4) How fast cars <u>run</u>	(5) How elephants <u>walk</u>	(6) How flowers <u>grow</u>

39. Using Adjectives on the Titanic

Quick Access Information ➜ Adjectives are words that describe nouns or pronouns.

★ Here is a list of *Titanic* parts and instruments. Your job is to discover two adjectives that describe that part of the instrument.

★ You may need to look up the word in a dictionary.

SHIP PART OR INSTRUMENT	ADJECTIVE 1	ADJECTIVE 2
1. bow		
2. stern		
3. steerage		
4. ballroom		
5. lifeboat		
6. galley		
7. anchor		
8. water		
9. crow's-nest		
10. midship		
11. poop deck		
12. sextant		
13. compass		
14. bridge		
15. propeller		
16. starboard		
17. keel		
18. cabins		
19. bilge		
20. davits		
21. upper class		
22. boiler room		
23. iceberg		
24. sea		
25. funnel		

Name_____ Date_____

40. Adverbs for Akira and Sonia

> **Quick Access Information** ➔ An adverb is a word that *modifies* a verb, an adjective, or another adverb. The word <u>modifies</u> means the adverb tells how, when, where, how far, how long, or to what extent or degree the verb, adjective, or other adverb is. Many adverbs end in *ly*, e.g., *Bighampton ran recklessly.* (<u>Recklessly</u> tells how Bighampton ran.)

★ Listed below are ten sentences. Your job is to pick out only one adverb from each sentence and write it in the first column. In the second column, place an adverb of your own that could replace the one in the sentence.

	ADVERB	NEW ADVERB
1. Sonia came quickly to kill the mice after Akira screamed.		
2. They romped so happily she hated to do it.		
3. Akira was safely up on his chair.		
4. "See how they run furiously," Akira cried.		
5. Surprisingly, the mice appeared to be completely blind.		
6. Sonia, being a farmer's wife, knew how to correctly use a carving knife.		
7. Wisely, she only cut off their tails.		
8. This bothered the mice only temporarily and without pain.		
9. "I couldn't kill them," Sonia said, "that would hurt me emotionally."		
10. Fearfully Akira blurted, "Did you ever see such a sight in your life as three blind mice?"		

I'M ALL RIGHT, EVERYBODY!

Name_____ Date _____

41. Pronouns with Molly Sousa and Flipper Twerpski

Quick Access Information ➔ A word used in place of or instead of a noun is called a pronoun. The pronoun must agree with the word or phrase it refers to (its antecedent) in terms of gender, person, and number.

★ Choose the correct pronouns from the Choice Box to fit into the spaces in the following story. Be sure to capitalize when necessary!

Once upon a time there was a friendly student named Molly Sousa. _____ decided to sell _____ collection of teenage magazines. _____ made a deal with Flipper Twerpski who was somewhat of a sneaky character. _____ talked Molly into taking the sum of two supposedly magic beans for _____ collection of awesome teen magazines. _____ was upset when _____ heard how Flipper had gypped _____ friend, Molly.

That year was Molly's last year at _____ business school. _____ felt totally embarrassed because of the poor deal with the beans so _____ threw _____ out the window of the school. Instantly a huge beanstalk began to grow furiously, shaking the ground around Molly and _____ friends. The beanstalk began to shape itself into a ladder. Molly began to climb _____. When _____ reached the top, _____ saw a huge sign that said "Welcome to Giant Inc. _____ Have Just Climbed the Corporate Ladder of Success." Molly was offered an executive position with stock options. _____ soon cornered the market in the bean industry and bought several Ferraris.

Remember Flipper Twerpski? _____ became _____ executive assistant.

CHOICE BOX

everyone	her	she	she
he	her	she	their
he	her	she	them
her	it	she	they
her	she	she	you

45

42. Plurals of Nouns

QUICK ACCESS
information

Regular plurals are created by:

- Adding an "s" to the singular form of the noun.
  dog → dogs

- Adding "es" to the singular form of the noun if it ends in *ch, sh, s, x,* or *z*.
  class → classes

  "Z" also requires that the "z" be doubled.
  quiz → quizzes

- Changing "y" to "i" and adding "es" for nouns ending in *y* preceded by a consonant.
  lady → ladies

- Adding "s" to nouns ending in *y* preceded by a vowel.
  boy → boys

- Changing the "f" or "fe" in nouns ending in those letters to "ves."
  calf → calves; wife → wives

- Adding "s" to nouns ending in *o* preceded by a vowel.
  video → videos

- Adding "es" to some nouns ending in *o* preceded by a consonant.
  tomato → tomatoes

- Adding "s" to the most important noun of compound nouns.
  mother-in-law → mothers-in-law

- Adding "en" or "ren" to certain words.
  ox → oxen; child → children

- Changing the internal lettering of a noun.
  foot → feet

- Not changing some nouns.
  deer → deer

- Leaving some nouns spelled as they are because they have no singular form.
  pants → pants

43. Plural Puzzle: Part One

★ Study the words in the Choice Box. Choose the correct plural to fit each answer box.

1. Very young group of people

2. Persons we honor or copy

3. More than one calf

4. The plural of pig

5. More than one ox

6. The plural of female adult persons

7. More than one lady

8. Several rodents smaller than rats

9. A group of young male persons

10. The plural of dolly

CHOICE BOX

boys	dollies	mice	selves
calves	heroes	oxen	teeth
children	ladies	pigs	women

44. Plural Puzzle: Part Two

★ The clues consist of singular nouns. The puzzle requires you to think of the plural form of each noun and place it in the correct location on the puzzle.

ACROSS

3. mail
4. child
7. bear
8. rodent
10. sheep
12. ox
13. mouse
14. tomato
16. foot
18. elf
19. hero

DOWN

1. lady
2. wife
4. church
5. deer
6. one
9. self
11. potato
15. calf
17. toe

45. Making Nouns Plural: Part One

★ Make the following nouns plural in the column on the right.

NOUN	PLURAL FORM
1. truck	
2. joystick	
3. monitor	
4. birch	
5. loaf	
6. piano	
7. plus	
8. baby	
9. class	
10. writer in residence	
11. jockey	
12. scarf	
13. radio	
14. potato	
15. ox	
16. pants	
17. oddity	
18. child	
19. witch	
20. camel	

46. Making Nouns Plural: Part Two

★   Make the following nouns plural in the column on the right.

NOUN	PLURAL FORM
1. daughter-in-law	
2. life	
3. loaf	
4. sleigh	
5. monster	
6. Internet	
7. moss	
8. turkey	
9. sheep	
10. leaf	
11. city	
12. tooth	
13. calf	
14. lamp	
15. horse	
16. lemon	
17. monkey	
18. lady-in-waiting	
19. queen	
20. fear	

Name_____ Date _____

47. Collective Nouns

Quick Access Information ➔ A word like "team" is called a *collective noun*. This collective noun is actually a group of persons or things and is seen to be singular or considered as one thing. It has no singular form.

★ Circle the collective nouns in the following sentences.

1. The class was laughing at Bighampton.

2. The town council worried about Bighampton getting his driver's license.

3. The school was in a tizzy about it.

4. A bouquet of flowers was sent to his mother because everyone knew she was worried.

5. Some people even warned the Naval Fleet.

6. The regiment at the army base was warned to be ready.

7. A squadron of police helicopters was put on alert.

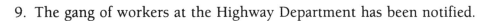

8. "Perhaps he should only drive a team of horses," Breanna suggested.

9. The gang of workers at the Highway Department has been notified.

10. The antique car club was told to watch for Bighampton.

11. The group of Boston police will never be the same.

12. The union of police fought for better wages after Bighampton received his license.

13. We have a plethora of smart student drivers in our city, but then came Bighampton Butler Jones.

14. The organization of Mothers Against Bighampton tried to deal with the problem.

15. The safety committee arranged for Bighampton to put a siren on his car to warn people.

48. Contractions—The Long and the Short of It

> **Quick Access Information** ➔ A contraction is the shortened form of a word or phrase. An apostrophe is put in place of the letter or letters that are left out.

★ Choose the correct contraction from the Great Contraction Sack and place it in the appropriate spot in Column B to match the words in Column A.

COLUMN A	COLUMN B
1. have not	
2. he has	
3. you are	
4. they are	
5. who is	
6. will not	
7. do not	
8. he would	
9. can not	
10. she will	
11. it is	
12. I am	
13. are not	
14. let us	
15. we have	

it's   I'm
we've   can't   you're
they're   aren't   she'll
who's   haven't
won't   let's   he'd
he's   don't

The Great
Contraction
Sack

Name_____ Date _____

49. Contraction Use in Sentences

Quick Access Information ➔ A contraction is the shortened form of a word or phrase. An apostrophe is put in place of the letter or letters that are left out.

★ Choose a contraction from The Great Contraction Sack to fit in the appropriate space in each sentence. Each contraction is used only once.

1. _____ you seen Bighampton this week?

2. _____ moved from Tulsa to Boise.

3. _____ go to New York on Thursday.

4. _____ win a million dollars if she goes on the show.

5. _____ you be my valentine?

6. _____ you ready yet?

7. _____ a girl!

8. _____ bug me!

9. _____ I have another ice cream cone?

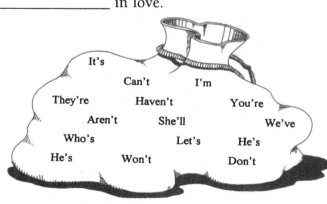

10. _____ the one you love?

11. _____ the most lovely couple.

12. _____ the best friend a person could have.

13. _____ stronger than Hercules.

14. _____ beat you in an arm wrestle.

15. _____ in love.

It's
Can't   I'm
They're   Haven't   You're
Aren't   She'll   We've
Who's   Let's   He's
He's   Won't   Don't

The Great
Contraction
Sack

Name_____ Date_____

50. The Great Abbreviation Page

★ Listed below are a series of abbreviations or shortened forms of words.

★ Match the abbreviation to its long form by drawing a line from the abbreviation on the left to its long form on the right. NOTE: Some abbreviations can have more than one long form.

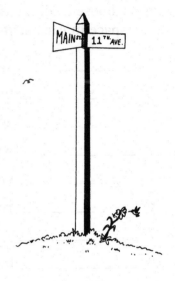

Dr.	Reverend
Mr.	Way
Mrs.	Road
St.	Mister
Ave.	Valley
Rd.	Mistress (married woman)
VLY	Lane
LN	Street
Ct.	Miss or Mrs.
Wy.	Canada or Chartered Accountant or California
Blvd.	Doctor
NE	Nebraska
Rev.	Rural Route or Railroad
Ms.	Apartment
RR	Boulevard
USA	Court
CA	Avenue
Apt.	United States of America

51. Choosing Synonyms—Words that Mean the Same

★ Write the word from the Choice Box that means the same or almost the same as the words given as clues.

CLUES	MY ANSWERS
1. trash, junk, debris, rubble	_____
2. car, machine, hot rod	_____
3. inquire, pry into, explore	_____
4. drunk, inebriated, tipsy	_____
5. creation, fabrication	_____
6. ugly, repulsive, gruesome	_____
7. laughable, amusing, gleeful	_____
8. paradise, an idyllic place	_____
9. prohibited, taboo, denied	_____
10. stranger, outsider, alien	_____
11. energy, power, punch	_____
12. brawling, conflict, combat	_____
13. crookedness, deceit, skulduggery	_____
14. ebony, jet, raven	_____
15. twist, curve, bow	_____
16. good looks, elegance, charm, polish	_____
17. creature, beast, livestock	_____
18. fury, rage, snarl, wrath	_____
19. entertainment, diversion, recreation	_____
20. entertainer, performer, player, star	_____

CHOICE BOX

anger	bend	fighting	amusement	actor
rubbish	automobile	force	investigate	foreigner
beauty	intoxicated	black	hilarious	heaven
dishonesty	hideous	animal	forbidden	invention

52. The Difference Among Synonyms, Homonyms, and Antonyms

QUICK ACCESS
information

Quick Access Information ➔ A synonym is a word that means the same as or close to another word. A homonym is a word that sounds the same as another word but has a different meaning. An antonym is a word that has the opposite meaning to another word.

★ On the lines below, write "S" for those pairs that are synonyms, "A" for antonyms, and "H" for homonyms.

1. ____ fun, thrills

2. ____ bare, bear

3. ____ raise, lower

4. ____ tall, short

5. ____ long, brief

6. ____ now, then

7. ____ plane, plain

8. ____ to, too

9. ____ go, stop

10. ____ move, proceed

11. ____ come, return

12. ____ war, peace

13. ____ sharp, dull

14. ____ wide, narrow

15. ____ smart, intelligent

16. ____ deep, shallow

17. ____ rain, reign

18. ____ gate, gait

19. ____ cellar, attic

20. ____ went, gone

21. ____ dollar, money

22. ____ bate, bait

23. ____ talk, conversation

24. ____ horns, antlers

25. ____ smooth, rough

26. ____ good, well

27. ____ pig, hog

28. ____ knew, new

29. ____ elephant, pachyderm

30. ____ friends, pals

31. ____ worry, anxiety

32. ____ foolish, wise

33. ____ blew, blue

34. ____ dead, alive

35. ____ wind, breeze

36. ____ sound, noise

37. ____ sea, see

38. ____ easy, hard

39. ____ polite, rude

40. ____ eager, apathetic

41. ____ lady, gentleman

42. ____ easy, hard

43. ____ drove, rode

44. ____ red, scarlet

SAY! THIS GIVES ME AN IDEA.

Name_____ Date_____

53. The Wonderful Antonym Puzzle

★ The words to be found in Puzzle A have antonyms or word opposites in Puzzle B.

★ The words and their antonyms begin at the same place on each puzzle, but some words have longer or shorter antonyms.

★ Circle the word in Puzzle A or B and circle its antonym in the other puzzle.

★ Write the correct antonyms next to the words listed below. Some are found in Puzzle A and some are found in Puzzle B.

PUZZLE A

```
L A R G E S M O T I O N T
H G I V E M A S C N S A D
P I B L O V E C O L D T Y
O X N J Q U I D M T U E S
W E N D B N I M E T G A A
E N M P E X C I T I N G F
R E F E F I N D M E R H E
B E C R Y M E P M Y E I T
R H O R R I B L E M K U Y
E B B D F L A H A P P Y E
B E R F E C X P A R D O N
D A U G H T E R A V O I D
H I N T E L L I G E N C E
```

PUZZLE B

```
S M A L L A S T I L L X T
H T A K E V B O G S J O Y
W H I H A T E H O T C H I
E X T R R O P R M B E R D
A U B P K Z I N U R D E A
K U P O B O R I N G I D N
N I L R L O S E R Z N L G
E P L A U G H P N O P M E
S L O V E L Y E P O I K R
S V E T R N R A N G R Y M
M P F O L F Y C H A R G E
S O N U O P W Y M E E T S
S I G N O R A N C E R E T
```

1. large _____
2. still _____
3. boring _____
4. charge _____
5. calm _____
6. avoid _____
7. happy _____
8. danger _____
9. intelligence _____
10. soft _____

11. come _____
12. lovely _____
13. laugh _____
14. give _____
15. power _____
16. love _____
17. son _____
18. find _____
19. cold _____
20. joy _____

54. Overworked, Tired, and Worn-out Synonyms

★ Look at the tired, overworked, and worn-out words below and think of a word that means the same as the word in the list.

★ Place the new word from the Choice Box in the proper space in the puzzle that corresponds or goes with the number of the tired word.

TIRED-WORD BOX

1. pretty	4. terrible	7. honest	10. fun	13. smart
2. okay	5. walk	8. excited	11. anger	14. happy
3. mean	6. fill	9. bad	12. fear	15. leap

CHOICE BOX

amusement	glad	horrid	rage	sincere
dread	gorgeous	nasty	satisfactory	stroll
frenzied	hop	occupy	sharp	wicked

Name_____ Date _____

55. Picking "P"-Word Synonyms Perfectly

★ Circle the word or phrase in each line that gives the closest meaning to the underlined word.

1. pocketbook: **(a)** horse **(b)** purse **(c)** rubber boot

2. plunge: **(a)** dive **(b)** hit **(c)** dog

3. plumage: **(a)** chicken **(b)** feathers **(c)** ostrich

4. plead: **(a)** yell **(b)** hate **(c)** implore

5. plaza: **(a)** ivory tower **(b)** village green **(c)** shopping mall

6. plunder: **(a)** give **(b)** sneak **(c)** ravage

7. portly: **(a)** skinny **(b)** corpulent **(c)** wild

8. pose: **(a)** stance **(b)** run **(c)** sleep

9. poverty: **(a)** wealth **(b)** impoverishment **(c)** cheap

10. postulate: **(a)** hypothesis **(b)** guess **(c)** anger

11. practical: **(a)** elephants **(b)** dogs **(c)** useful

12. predilection: **(a)** leaning **(b)** preference **(c)** nasty

13. preamble: **(a)** scramble **(b)** power **(c)** introduction

14. precious: **(a)** valuable **(b)** penny-wise **(c)** cute

15. premises: **(a)** doghouse **(b)** home fires **(c)** grounds

16. prosecute: **(a)** put on trial **(b)** judge **(c)** jury

17. proponent: **(a)** supporter **(b)** depression **(c)** tigers

18. phony: **(a)** CD player **(b)** paint **(c)** fraud

19. perturb: **(a)** cats **(b)** disturb **(c)** upset

20. placid: **(a)** lake in CA **(b)** peaceful **(c)** cows

21. podium: **(a)** coat rack **(b)** plateau **(c)** soap box

22. plutocracy: **(a)** rich wealthy class **(b)** poor people **(c)** plebians

23. plumb: **(a)** slant **(b)** vertical **(c)** horizontal

24. plot: **(a)** hospital **(b)** coffin **(c)** scheme

25. pluck: **(a)** pick or gather **(b)** throw away **(c)** bury

56. The Homonym Puzzle

Quick Access Information ➡ Homonyms are words that sound the same but have different meanings.

★ Circle the homonym of each word below as you find it in the puzzle. Write each word beside its homonym in the space provided.

B	S	E	M	N	P	O	L	W	Q	U	H	P	O	M	B	L	N	I
N	J	G	N	H	I	L	U	W	A	L	O	U	D	N	L	H	F	G
B	I	L	P	O	R	W	E	S	T	D	U	M	V	W	I	U	L	K
K	L	O	M	P	C	N	M	D	E	E	R	W	C	D	R	E	W	M
T	R	W	I	V	S	B	M	R	I	O	S	R	V	U	E	N	A	C
R	G	H	M	T	E	M	B	U	G	E	Y	V	B	M	W	A	I	T
N	L	K	S	J	E	B	T	E	H	B	W	H	O	L	E	V	S	R
Y	W	K	J	K	N	I	G	H	T	P	O	E	I	M	E	N	T	O
P	L	A	I	N	Y	W	X	E	R	T	E	A	W	C	K	P	V	W
I	C	W	L	O	R	B	B	A	R	E	V	L	D	E	V	R	I	P
X	K	N	E	W	E	S	B	R	U	A	K	L	E	V	C	I	D	R
C	R	W	A	J	L	E	A	D	O	M	R	W	C	A	N	T	I	B
K	E	L	P	E	W	A	M	T	L	N	O	L	S	C	W	E	T	L

allowed _____	herd _____	ore _____	tee _____
ate _____	hole _____	ours _____	teem _____
aunt _____	led _____	plane _____	two _____
bear _____	new _____	right _____	waste _____
dear _____	night _____	scene _____	weak _____
heel _____	no _____	see _____	weight _____

Name_____ Date_____

57. Two-Function Synonym Puzzle

★ Search each box for *five* 4- and 5-letter words that are synonyms of each other and circle them. The words can be found forward, backward, and diagonally.

★ Write the words in alphabetical order on the lines beside each box.

F	E	A	R	B	C	I
R	P	M	L	O	P	W
W	T	Y	B	A	P	D
O	O	H	N	K	R	E
R	F	I	G	E	C	M
R	C	N	A	R	I	N
Y	G	D	Y	T	V	S

_____

_____

_____

_____

_____

F	B	M	A	Q	P	D
U	A	S	C	U	K	R
I	J	S	W	I	F	T
A	S	R	T	C	L	B
B	R	I	S	K	M	Y
M	R	A	P	I	D	L
E	N	V	C	W	O	P

_____

_____

_____

_____

_____

W	L	B	N	O	S	G
P	V	A	W	A	L	F
C	W	M	P	N	I	A
J	L	K	I	S	P	U
E	P	D	Y	H	E	L
B	U	N	F	H	G	T
W	E	R	R	O	R	J

_____

_____

_____

_____

_____

58. Synonym and Antonym Grids

★ **This page is a little different. You will enjoy it. Discover the contents of the grid puzzles below and write your answers on the lines. The words can be found forward, backward, and diagonally.**

1. Circle the three synonyms and three antonyms for the word <u>hard</u> in the grid puzzle below.

R	F	A	C	V	W	N	P	S	P	M	T
L	I	M	P	N	A	U	S	H	M	B	E
A	R	G	W	K	P	I	G	O	R	J	N
O	M	H	I	L	M	U	J	D	F	W	D
N	I	T	B	D	O	W	R	T	P	T	E
V	P	E	R	T	R	E	O	A	S	B	R

SYNONYMS   ANTONYMS

_____   _____

_____   _____

_____   _____

2. Circle the four synonyms and four antonyms for the word <u>bad</u> in the grid puzzle below.

B	E	N	A	S	T	Y	W	O	P	K	E
G	A	W	F	U	L	G	N	E	M	L	R
R	O	T	T	E	N	J	O	R	V	U	M
E	M	A	V	T	I	K	T	O	T	I	P
A	K	O	C	Y	C	P	Y	S	D	S	L
T	L	P	W	M	E	L	N	O	E	W	U

SYNONYMS   ANTONYMS

_____   _____

_____   _____

_____   _____

_____   _____

3. Circle the three synonyms and five antonyms for the word <u>freedom</u> in the grid puzzle below.

L	O	C	K	U	P	R	T	A	G	U	H
E	G	A	C	J	A	I	L	R	T	N	S
O	P	K	E	R	M	V	N	R	V	T	D
L	I	B	E	R	T	Y	S	E	W	I	C
U	W	V	E	B	D	G	F	S	D	E	M
S	Y	P	R	I	S	O	N	T	W	T	N

SYNONYMS   ANTONYMS

_____   _____

_____   _____

_____   _____

_____

59. Compound Words

Quick Access Information ➜ A compound word is made from two or more words joined together to form a new word.

★ Pick a word from the Choice Box to combine with the words in each row. The word you choose will make compound words. Place the word in the space provided. The first one is completed for you.

1. noon	hours	life	math	**after**
2. wheel	under	logged	melon	
3. bell	grass	bonnet	print	
4. brush	do	line	cut	
5. every	self	any	time	
6. wood	catcher	house	tired	
7. port	plane	men	food	
8. field	space	craft	plane	
9. sick	nest	true	bird	
10. black	song	brain	bath	
11. boat	cleaner	hold	fly	
12. cracker	storm	arm	back	
13. will	style	wheel	way	
14. fish	nip	tom	tail	
15. bed	watch	blow	trap	

CHOICE BOX

cat	love	after	free	water
fire	sea	death	blue	bird
hair	house	dog	one	air

60. Developing Compound Words

★ Match a word or letter in Column A with a word in Column B to make a totally new word for Column C. You may use the words in Column B more than once. The first one is completed for you.

	A		B	C
1.	steam		walking	steamboat
2.	horse		spread	
3.	keep		bred	
4.	base		house	
5.	life		teller	
6.	wrong		hang	
7.	sweet		ball	
8.	mail		person	
9.	thorough		boat	
10.	zig		sight	
11.	doll		shoe	
12.	team		glass	
13.	story		hole	
14.	spy		place	
15.	over		hopper	
16.	loop		bound	
17.	snow		guard	
18.	wheel		sake	
19.	sleep		making	
20.	bed		barrow	
21.	common		doing	
22.	merry		zag	
23.	safe		work	
24.	sales		heart	
25.	grass		box	

Name_____ Date_____

61. Compound Sets

★ Listed below are sets of unrelated words or phrases.

★ Your task is to find a suitable word from the Choice Box that comes before each word in the set.

★ Write the suitable word on the line at the end of each set.

1.	board	dose	dress	haul	_____
2.	post	rage	smart	law	_____
3.	shine	light	beam	burn	_____
4.	ground	drop	board	gammon	_____
5.	out	made	cuff	some	_____
6.	bird	sick	less	lorn	_____
7.	boat	hair	shot	hand	_____
8.	place	fighter	proof	storm	_____
9.	headed	hearted	weight	house	_____
10.	will	hand	loader	way	_____
11.	bed	cake	headed	foot	_____
12.	boat	hold	coat	fly	_____
13.	house	horn	land	back	_____
14.	ware	wood	ship	board	_____
15.	light	ache	first	long	_____

CHOICE BOX

back	green	head	light	out
fire	hand	hot	long	over
free	hard	house	love	sun

62. Constructing Compound Words

★ Listed below are sets of unrelated words. The words on the same line require the same word to make them compound. Choose a suitable word for each line from the Choice Box below. The first one is done for you.

1. ___**over**___board   ___**over**___ripe   ___**over**___eager

2. _____post   _____pour   _____law

3. _____struck   _____light   _____gaze

4. _____man   _____box   _____room
    (person)

5. _____bag   _____made   _____cart

6. _____bird   _____struck   _____lorn

7. _____boat   _____bow   _____horn

8. _____stone   _____ache   _____board

9. _____dog   _____cake   _____head

10. _____boat   _____coat   _____fly

11. _____horn   _____house   _____grocer

12. _____ball   _____up   _____headed

CHOICE BOX

green	hand	hard	head
hot	house	long	love
mail	out	~~over~~	star

Name_____ Date_____

63. Making the Most of Similes

Quick Access Information ➔ When a writer or speaker uses "like" or "as" to make a comparison, that person is using a simile.

★ **Your job is to finish the following similes with words or expressions that would make good comparisons. Write your completed similes on another sheet of paper.**

1. As light as _____

2. Like the winds of the field, she _____

3. Jamalia is as tall as _____

4. Like sorrow, she _____

5. Dirty as _____

6. That guitar looks like _____

7. She is as cool as _____

8. That dog barks like _____

9. He is as lazy as _____

10. This pig smells like _____

11. She moves across the floor like _____

12. That alien looked like _____

13. He is as cute as _____

14. Breanna talks like _____

15. Bighampton's car looks like _____

16. Akira plays the drums like _____

17. My CD player skips like _____

18. That toad looks like _____

19. Her skin is as smooth as _____

20. Like the birds of the sky, she _____

21. Straight as _____

22. Strong as _____

23. Dark as _____

24. Crooked as _____

25. Old as _____

26. Sick as _____

27. It flowed like water off _____

28. Vernon was as green as _____

QUICK ACCESS
information

64. Making the Most of Metaphors

Quick Access Information ➔ When a writer or speaker compares by speaking of one thing as if it were another, that speaker or writer is using a metaphor.

★ Your task is to finish the following metaphors with words or expressions that would make good comparisons. Write your complete metaphors on another sheet of paper.

1. The full moon is a(n) _____.

2. Mountains are silent _____.

3. She is a real _____.

4. He is a real _____ when it comes to work.

5. An oak tree is a strong _____.

6. This room is a _____ stye.

7. This car is a(n) _____.

8. He's called an old _____.

9. A teenager's car can be a _____ pit.

10. He's a cunning _____.

11. She's a sly _____.

12. She is a sneaky _____.

13. Dale, don't make a(n) _____ of yourself.

14. The _____ is my hero.

15. All the world's a(n) _____.

16. Billy was _____ (afraid).

17. The house was a(n) _____ eyes.

18. I smell a _____ (rodent).

19. Don't be a(n) _____.

20. His _____ is a metaphor.

21. Carolyn and David are peas in the same _____.

22. She is a social _____ (colorful winged insect).

23. He's the _____ for tonight.

24. Actors are real _____.

25. Tell those _____ to stop fooling around.

65. Writing Conversation: Part One

- Words in a sentence that show exactly what a person says are called <u>quotations</u>.

- Quotation marks are used before and after the exact words spoken. These quotation marks are at the high point in the line where the quotation is. The first set looks like little 6's (") *before* the words spoken. The second set looks like little 9's (") *after* the words spoken and is called the rear set.

- A comma is used to separate the words spoken, the quotation, from the other words in the sentence.

- A capital letter always starts the first word of the quotation, no matter where it is in the sentence.

- **Quotation at the beginning or start of a sentence:** When the words spoken occur at the beginning of a sentence, you must place a comma inside the last set of quotation marks (,").

EXAMPLE:

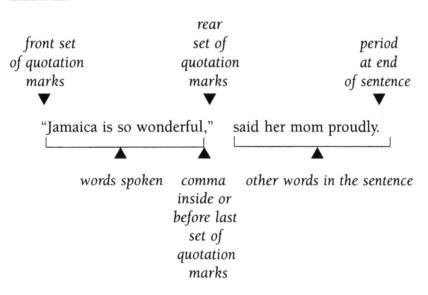

Copyright © 2002 by John Wiley & Sons, Inc.

QUICK ACCESS
information

66. Writing Conversation: Part Two

- **Quotation at the end of a sentence:** Words spoken in a sentence can come at the end of that sentence. In this case, you must place the comma *before* the first set of quotation marks (, ").

EXAMPLE

first set of quotation marks followed by a capital letter
▼

rear set of quotation marks
▼

Kathy said to her son, "Please eat your vegetables."

▲
comma before first set of quotation marks

▲
punctuation inside quotation marks

- When the quotation is in the form of a question, you must use a question mark (?) immediately after the words spoken.

- When the quotation is in the form of an exclamation, you must use an exclamation mark (!) immediately after the words spoken.

- The question mark or exclamation mark must be placed *inside* the rear set of quotation marks (?") or (!").

- When the quotation begins a sentence, the question mark or exclamation mark *takes the place of the comma.*

EXAMPLE

"Ouch!" said Bighampton.
▲
exclamation mark takes the place of the comma

EXAMPLE (**Quotations in question form**)

front set of quotation marks
▼

rear set of quotation marks
▼

"What are we eating?" asked Mabeline. ◄*period at the end*
▲
questions mark at end of words spoken (takes the place of the comma)

67. Writing Conversation: Part Three

QUICK ACCESS information

EXAMPLE (Quotations in exclamation form)

*front set of quotation
marks followed by
a capital letter* ▼   *rear set of quotation marks* ▼

Mabeline asked, "Does this soup taste funny to you?"

▲ *comma*   ▲ *question mark inside rear set
of quotation marks*

EXAMPLE (Quotations in exclamation form)

*front set of
quotation marks* ▼   *rear set of
quotation marks* ▼   *period at the end* ▼

"I've caught another rattlesnake!" shouted the cook.

▲ *exclamation mark at the end of the words spoken
(takes the place of the comma)*

EXAMPLE (Quotations in exclamation form)

*front set of quotation marks followed by
a capital letter* ▼   *rear set of quotation marks* ▼

Mabeline shouted excitedly, "There's something strange in my soup!"

▲ *comma*   ▲ *exclamation mark inside rear
set of quotation marks*

- **Divided quotations:** Quotations that are separated into two parts are called divided quotations. Quotation marks must be used before and after each spoken part of the divided quotation. A capital letter is used only at the start of the sentence and not for the first word in the second part. Commas are placed after the first part is spoken and after the speaker is identified.

*front set of
quotation marks* ▼   *middle sets of quotation marks* ▼   ▼   *last set of
quotation marks* ▼

EXAMPLE: "Don't sneeze too loudly," said Bighampton, "or you will wake the gorilla."

▲ *comma*   ▲ *comma*

68. Writing What Someone Says: Part One

★ In the sentences below, put quotation marks and commas in their proper places to show what the speaker is saying.

★ Underline the words that are not part of the conversation or words spoken. The first one has been done for you.

1. "Please give me the mirror," <u>asked Breanna</u>.

2. Give her the hairbrush and the mirror her boyfriend Bighampton timidly suggested.

3. I just wanted to see how pretty I am said Breanna.

4. You may be pretty but I'm smart Sonia blurted in defense.

5. We've got to do something about Breanna Mike said to Bighampton.

6. Yes she's got a big head Molly interjected.

7. Arrogant people turn me off said Mike.

8. When you're this pretty, it's easy to admire yourself Breanna interrupted.

9. I can't say much because I'm her boyfriend Bighampton said cowardly.

10. People should just admit and accept the fact that I'm a beautiful person Breanna said proudly.

11. This is hard to take Mike observed.

12. That's for sure everyone responded at the same time.

HOW SWEET IT IS.

Copyright © 2002 by John Wiley & Sons, Inc.

69. Writing What Someone Says: Part Two

★ Rewrite the sentences below on a separate sheet of paper, putting quotation marks, capitals, and commas in their proper places.

★ Underline the words that are not part of the conversation or words spoken.

★ The first one has been done for you.

1. <u>Bighampton thought for a while and then said</u>, "I don't want to go."

2. Akira replied you will never get another chance.

3. Karrie looked at the plane and stated you're frightened because this plane is over sixty years old.

4. Bighampton blurted I'm scared and I have a right to be.

5. Akira looked at his friends and said but it's been fully restored.

6. Bighampton, shaking with fear, said it's not the actual safe flying that bothers me.

7. Bighampton continued I'm more concerned about how the plane comes down.

8. Karrie looked at the large wings and said it is heavier than air.

9. Breanna looked at Bighampton and cooed will you do it for me?

10. Akira looked at Bighampton and mocked come on scaredy cat.

11. Karrie retorted I kind of agree with Bighampton.

12. Breathing a sigh of relief, Bighampton blurted I never argue with a lady who has the correct point of view.

70. Writing What Someone Says: Part Three

★ Rewrite each sentence below on the lines provided.

★ Place quotation marks, commas, periods, question marks, apostrophes, exclamation marks, and capital letters in their proper locations as you rewrite the sentence.

1. Are you waiting for bighampton asked akira

_____

2. Wow breanna you sure are strong blurted akira

_____

3. Breanna retorted are you teasing me

_____

4. Akira shouted suddenly dont move

_____

5. Akira asked may i take your picture

_____

6. Stop teasing me breanna shrieked

_____

7. Is bighampton back from his muscle-building workout breanna queried

_____

8. Just wait till i get my hands on him breanna grumbled

_____

9. Does he cater to your every whim and request akira asked

_____

10. He hasnt catered to every whim or request breanna replied once in grade five several years ago he didnt pick up a pencil for me

_____

_____

Name_____ Date_____

71. Writing What Someone Says: Part Four

★ Read the conversation below. This is the story of two fairy tale characters some fifty years after their original stories. They are both in the Sunny Vale Retirement Home.

★ Rewrite this conversation on another sheet of paper and put in the correct punctuation where necessary.

★ The first part has been completed to help you get started.

A DAY AT THE SUNNY VALE RETIREMENT HOME

"Hi, Big Bad," Mr. Bear stated. "How are you feeling today?"

"Oh, greetings, Mr. Bear," Big Bad Wolf replied, "my bones ache but other than that I'm okay."

Suddenly Mr. Bear blurted say do you remember the grief I had because of that little girl with the strange name

What do you mean strange name the Wolf cackled through his loose false teeth

Well Mr. Bear surmised how does Goldilocks sound to you

Big Bad Wolf pondered for a moment and said thats a strange name all right Come to think of it I had trouble with a little girl with a strange name too

What was it Mr. Bear asked.

Little Red Riding Hood Big Bad responded I also had some misfortune with three little pigs the Wolf went on but thats another story

Mr. Bear perked up and said I heard those three pigs are in the Cozy Sty Nursing Home on Pasadena Blvd What do you say we go over there and cause some trouble for old time's sake

Big Bad looked Mr. Bear in the face and said what with my rheumatism arthritis and lack of teeth Id sooner stay for dinner here in the home

Come to think of it Mr. Bear replied lets stay here and relax

SECTION 3

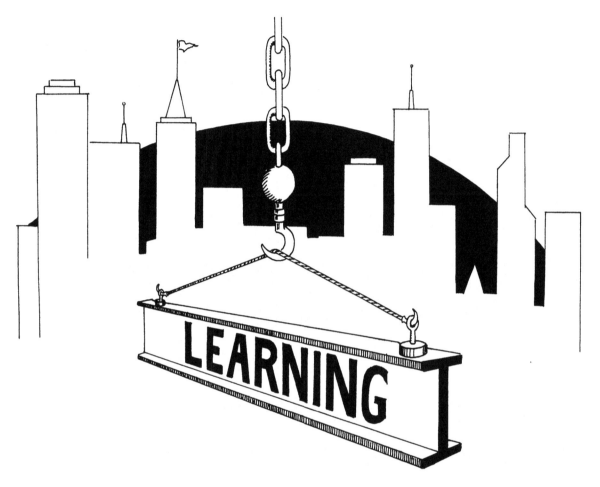

ENGLISH CONCEPTS AND TECHNIQUES TO STIMULATE AND ENRICH

Name_____ Date_____

72. Understanding Root, Prefix, and Suffix

Quick Access Information → A prefix is a syllable that comes *before* a root word. A suffix is a syllable that comes *after* a root word.

★ Your task is to identify the root as well as the suffix and/or prefix attached to each word listed.

★ Some prefixes are ex-, re-, un-, and dis-.

★ Some suffixes are -ly, -y, -ed, -er, and -ing.

WORD	ROOT	PREFIX	SUFFIX
unlovely			
lurching			
crusty			
ascertained			
perky			
lucky			
utterly			
uncluttered			
belabored			
unpublished			
shadowiness			
unhandy			
disapprove			
adventuring			
exchanged			
disliked			
returning			
anticlimax			
backer			
friskier			

73. Selfish Hyphenated Words

★ Each sentence below describes a word that begins with the word "self."

★ Choose a word from the Choice Box that is correctly described by each definition. Write the word in the space provided. A dictionary will help.

1. You have this when you like yourself _____

2. When you think you are more moral than others _____

3. You have this when you give up something for someone else's benefit

_____

4. This is an interest in your own well being _____

5. This is said about you when you seek everything for yourself _____

6. This occurs when you go without things you want _____

7. You are said to be this when you are worried about others' opinions about you

_____

8. When you think well of yourself, you have high . . . _____

9. When you teach yourself _____

10. When you can begin work without being told what to do _____

11. When a watch winds automatically _____

12. When you improve yourself _____

13. The gratification of your desires _____

14. Getting along without help _____

15. When you want and get your own way _____

Choice Box

self-conscious	self-interest	self-starter
self-denial	self-respect	self-supporting
self-esteem	self-righteous	self-taught
self-improvement	self-sacrifice	self-willed
self-indulgent	self-seeking	self-winding

74. Pretty "Pre" Words

★ Each sentence below describes a word that begins with the letters "pre."

★ Choose a word from the Choice Box that is correctly described by each definition. Write the word in the space provided. A dictionary will help.

1. This is exactness or when something is totally accurate _____

2. An idea, thought, or concept formed beforehand _____

3. An opinion formed when you do not take time to look at the situation properly

   beforehand _____

4. To get ready for something _____

5. To decide something beforehand; to determine prior to doing it

   _____

6. To say something is going to happen before it does _____

7. An unpleasant difficulty; a tight spot _____

8. The act of being very dominant _____

9. Standing above or ahead of everyone else _____

10. Rain _____

11. When something is valuable, it is this _____

12. A police district _____

13. A very steep drop off or cliff _____

14. Not safe and not secure situations _____

15. A clergyperson or minister _____

CHOICE BOX

preacher	precious	precise	predicament	predominate
precarious	precipice	preconception	predict	prejudice
precinct	precipitation	predetermined	predominance	prepare

Name_____ Date_____

75. Learning about Syllables

> **Quick Access Information** ➔ A syllable is a word or part of a word that is spoken as one unit or sound. It may be:
>
> 1. a vowel alone
> 2. a vowel with one or more consonants
>
> Sound out the word *American*. It has four syllables (A•mer•i•can).
> The word *park* has only one syllable (park).
> The name *Norman* has two syllables (Nor•man).

★ Your task is to read the story below and fill in the chart with one-, two-, and three-syllable words from the story. Separate the two- and three-syllable words with a dot between the syllables. One is done for you to help you get started.

Once upon a time there was this totally cool teenager named Bighampton Butler Jones. He was cool because he wore his cap backwards, had just the right clothes, and had plenty of hard cash.

Bighampton was walking in the woods one day when he thought to himself, "How nice it would be if I were a prince. I could eventually become a king and have everything I want." This was a great idea Bighampton surmised. "But how does a cool person like me become a prince?" he wondered. Suddenly Bighampton had a brainwave. "I'll kiss a frog; that should do it. I've heard of a person kissing a frog and instantly becoming a prince." Bighampton looked around and began kissing frogs he found in a nearby pond. He didn't realize, however, that his school biology class was on a field trip at the pond area and was observing Bighampton's strange behavior. After this event, Bighampton was having trouble being cool at school.

One-Syllable Words	Two-Syllable Words	Three-Syllable Words
		to•tal•ly

Name_____ Date_____

76. Proofreading for Capitals

Quick Access Information ➔ When you proofread you reread all the material you have written in order to correct mistakes.

★ Read the following sentences to discover which words need capital letters.

★ Draw a line through each small (lowercase) letter that should be a capital (uppercase) and write the correct capital above it.

For Example: ᴱelectonic games developed in ᴮboise, ᴵidaho are the best.

1. jamalia sousa was at the museum in cody, wyoming.

2. eugene aulinger is the best conductor of bernstein i have ever seen.

3. rick benson's composition of the musical piece called riel is a masterpiece.

4. "the video game, *power blasted doorbells*, just rings my chimes," said bighampton.

5. the missouri river flows near billings, montana.

6. the ship uss *united states* must begin stopping twenty-five miles from new york.

7. karrie and i went to the chinese olympic games.

8. the anthony hotel was saved by the newport news fire department.

9. bighampton, the president of the largest class, has the biggest heart.

10. mandy, diane, gene, and james belong to a lovely family in louisiana.

11. bighampton went around with santa claus on december twenty-fourth.

12. in canada, bighampton found it slightly cool on santa's sleigh.

13. santa visited asia, north america, europe, and australia in about three hours on christmas eve.

14. bighampton flew the sleigh from boston to san francisco in the twinkling of an eye.

15. when they left boston, santa shouted, "this is the home of the best hockey team of all time."

77. Identifying Kinds of Sentences

Quick Access Information ➔ Sentences are grouped into four *kinds* according to their meaning.

A. The first one is a DECLARATIVE sentence. A declarative sentence makes a statement or just tells you something and ends in a period. (Kathy has a sore toe.)

B. The second kind is an INTERROGATIVE sentence. This kind of sentence *asks a question* and ends with a question mark. (Does Kathy have a sore toe?)

C. The third kind is an EXCLAMATORY sentence. This kind of sentence shows *surprise* or *excitement* and ends with an exclamation mark. (Wow, have you ever got a sore toe, Kathy!)

D. The fourth kind is the IMPERATIVE sentence. This kind of sentence makes a command and usually ends with a period. (Kathy, go to the doctor right now.)

★ **Listed below are ten sentences. Put the proper punctuation and write the kind of sentence it is at the end of each sentence.**

1. Get out of here__   _____

2. Was Bighampton mean to Vinny__   _____

3. What a horrible day Vinny had__   _____

4. Vinny did not have the best of luck__   _____

5. He thought he found a black-and-white cat__   _____

6. Watch out for that skunk__   _____

7. Did Vinny know it was a skunk__   _____

8. Vinny doesn't smell very good__   _____

9. Will he have to bathe in tomato juice__   _____

10. Wow, he sure smells bad__   _____

78. Punctuation

When to use a period   (.)

- After a sentence that tells you something. This is called a declarative sentence. (**The horse was white.**)

- After an initial or an abbreviation. (**J. P. Jones** or **Dr. Jones**)

When to use a question mark   (?)

- After a sentence that asks a question. This is called an interrogative sentence. (**Does Vinny have a video game?**)

When to use an exclamation point   (!)

- At the end of a sentence that shows excitement. This is called an exclamatory sentence. (**Look at the falling rock!**)

- After an interjection. (**Oh! Hurray! Ah!**)

When to use a comma   (,)

- To separate a quotation from a sentence. (**I said, "Hi there."**)

- After words like yes or no at the start of a sentence when they do not show strong feeling. (**No, I don't have an opinion.**)

- To separate words in a group or series. (**pigs, ducks, cows**)

- Between the name of a village, town, or city and the name of the state. (**Boise, Idaho**)

- After a person's family name when it precedes the initials of the first name. (**Tilford, M.**)

- After the greeting and at the complimentary close of a letter. (**Dear Tyler, Sincerely yours,**)

- Between the day, month, and year in a letter or other writing. (**Wednesday, May 14, 2007**)

- To separate words like *too, however, moreover, anywhere* in a sentence. (**I did not vote for my friend, however, when I learned his views.**)

When to use an apostrophe   (')

- When you have a contraction. (**isn't**)

- When you are showing ownership or possession. (**Tyler's video game**)

79. Showing Separate and Joint Possession

> **Quick Access Information** ➝ When two or more persons, places, or things have possession (ownership) of something individually, you use an apostrophe ('s). For example, <u>Bartel's and Johnson's reports were well presented.</u>
> ➝ When two or more persons, places, or things have possession (ownership) together, the apostrophe ('s) is used after the final owner of the object. For example, <u>We bought our elephant from Bartel and Johnson's Circus.</u>

★ **Show possession in these sentences by rewriting each sentence in the space provided.**

1. Bill and Larry dogs are gentle and kind.

   _____

2. Esther admired Alan and Wanda house.

   _____

3. Esther and her husband farm is wonderful.

   _____

4. Marlene and her friend Carol drawings have a professional touch.

   _____

5. Yesterday we went to Peter and Mary homes.

   _____

6. Maggie and her sister truck was full.

   _____

7. The doctor and the staff responses were terrific.

   _____

8. Marlene and Carol new cars both had bad dents.

   _____

9. We visited the display at Johnson and Wilson market.

   _____

10. Why did you not want Smith and Henry new Ferrari?

   _____

Name _____ Date _____

80. Possessive Singular and Possessive Plural

Quick Access Information ➜ Possession by an individual is shown by adding 's, e.g., <u>lady's handbag</u>. Possession by a group is shown by adding ' to the plural form of the word, e.g., <u>ladies' handbags</u>.

★ Complete the chart below. The first one is done for you.

SINGULAR	POSSESSIVE SINGULAR	POSSESSIVE PLURAL
1. lady handbag	lady's handbag	ladies' handbags
2. elephant trunk		
3. hive queen		
4. cowgirl hat		
5. tiger tail		
6. secretary desk		
7. mother-in-law cane		
8. Esther last name		
9. orange flavor		
10. wife paycheck		
11. box lid		
12. knife blade		
13. doctor bill		
14. nurse uniform		
15. patient gown		

Name _____ Date _____

81. "Person" of Nouns

Quick Access Information ➔ The "person" of a noun indicates one of three things:

1. The *first* person is the *speaker* in a sentence.
2. The *second* person is the person spoken *to*.
3. The *third* person is the person or thing spoken *about*.

★ Read the sentences below and indicate on the line before each one the "person" (first, second, or third) of the noun that is in italics.

1. _____ *I* am coming.

2. _____ *Tony* is the coolest person in college.

3. _____ *Christa* has wonderful parents and a terrific brother.

4. _____ *Karrie,* we are happy to welcome you into our family.

5. _____ Have you ever seen the *street rod*?

6. _____ Pigs share the area of their *sty*.

7. _____ *Mrs. Watson,* I admire your daughter.

8. _____ The shop *teacher* was Mr. Tsutsumi.

9. _____ *Diamond* is a good cutter of glass.

10. _____ There were *sleds* at the dog race.

11. _____ Jazz is a form of *music* that expresses emotion.

12. _____ Kara was *head scientist* at the "Speed Talking Institute."

13. _____ *We* good-looking people must not be arrogant.

14. _____ The *group* works in the market.

15. _____ *I* am simply exhausted.

Name_____ Date _____

82. Where Are the Vowels?

★ Insert the missing vowels (A, E, I, O, U) in the story below in order to make it complete and understandable.

H. DUMPTY THE TEENEGGER

__n_ d__y H__mpty D__mpty d__c__d__d t__ d__ s__m__
s__r__ __ __s s__tt__ng.

H__s m__m s__ __d, "Y__ __ c__n't d__ s__r__ __ __s s__tt__ng.
Y__ __'r__ t__ __ r__ __nd__d __n th__ b__tt__m. S__n, y__ __'r__ j__st
t__ __ __v__l."

"D__n't w__rry __b__ __t m__, M__m. __'m __ t__ __n__gg__r
n__w, __nd __ d__n't n__ __d t__ l__st__n t__ __ld scr__mbl__d
__d__ __s," h__ r__t__rt__d pr__ __dly.

W__th th__ __t th__ c__nf__d__nt H__mpty w__nt __ff t__ f__nd __
s__r__ __ __s s__tt__ng __dv__nt__r__.

__t f__rst h__ tr__ __d s__v__r__l pl__c__s. H__ w__s t__ __
w__d__ t__ s__t __n __ sk__t__b__ __rd __r sc__ __t__r __nd th__
v__d__ __ p__rl__r w__s j__st t__ __ n__ __sy. F__n__lly, wh__l__
w__lk__ng __l__ng __nd w__nd__r__ng why h__s p__r__nts w__ __ld
n__m__ __ k__d H__mpty __n th__ f__rst pl__c__, h__ sp__ __d th__
p__rf__ct sp__t. __t w__s __ st__n__ w__ll.

"__h, h__!" h__ bl__rt__d. "L__t th__ s__r__ __ __s s__tt__ng
__dv__nt__r__ b__g__n." __s h__ n__stl__d d__wn __n t__p __f th__
w__ll, h__ c__ __ld s__ __ s__m__b__dy c__m__ng. L__ __n__ng f__rw__rd
t__ s__ __ __nd n__t __w__r__ h__ w__s l__s__ng h__s gr__p, h__
s__ __d, "H__, k__ng's h__rs__s __nd k__ng's m__n." S__dd__nly,
__ __ps . . . __nd th__ r__st __s h__st__ry.

89

83. Capitalization Skills

★ Rewrite the paragraph below in the space provided.

★ Place capital letters in their proper locations.

★ Answer the Extra Credit Question at the bottom of the page.

A MYSTERY

several years ago little miss muffet was said to have sat on a tuffet eating curds and whey. breanna buckingham told jamalia sousa in boston that curds and whey were the solid and watery parts of milk. a mystery remains, however, as to what a tuffet is. bighampton butler jones from scranton thinks it is a toadstool, but he is not sure. no dictionary, not even the famous peterson's dictionary, has the definition of a tuffet. perhaps we should hire the zip detective service to solve the mystery. the whole world wants to have the answer to this burning question, "what is a tuffet?"

_____

_____

_____

_____

_____

_____

_____

_____

_____

_____

_____

EXTRA CREDIT QUESTION: What do you think a tuffet could be?

84. Verb Tenses: Part One

> **Quick Access Information** ➜ Tenses of verbs tell "when" things happen. The three tenses most often used are present, past, and future.
>
> *Present:*   The action is happening now.
> *Past:*   The action has already happened.
> *Future:*   The action has not happened yet.

★ **Read the sentences below, then write** *present, past,* **or** *future* **after each one to indicate its tense.**

1. The hare and the tortoise prepared for the race yesterday. _____

2. They will know about the prize at the end. _____

3. Tickets for the race were all sold out last week. _____

4. We know Hairy the Hare and Tom Tortoise are dedicated. _____

5. They both know all there is to know about running. _____

6. Don the Donkey starts the race properly. _____

7. Hairy the Hare took an early lead. _____

8. The tortoise is my favorite right now. _____

9. You will win a big trophy when you reach the Finish line. _____

10. I am going crazy with power. _____

11. I shall sing of my glory and power. _____

12. I am the best, the greatest, and the fastest. _____

13. Hairy spotted his favorite resting spot an hour ago. _____

14. Hairy had a little snooze. _____

15. I will win if I don't stop. _____

16. Hairy thinks to himself, "You are so cool." _____

17. Hairy the Hare continued to snooze on and on, missing the end of the race.

_____

18. "You've made it," Tamara the Turtle said to Tom the Tortoise, "you've won the race."

_____

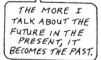

BIGHAMPTON, YOU LOOK TENSE.

THE MORE I TALK ABOUT THE FUTURE IN THE PRESENT, IT BECOMES THE PAST.

Name_____ Date_____

85. Verb Tenses: Part Two

Quick Access Information → Tenses of verbs tell "when" things happen. The three tenses most often used are:

The *present* where the action is happening now.
The *past* where the action has already happened.
The *future* where the action has not happened yet.

★ Write *past, present,* or *future* after each sentence to indicate its tense.

1. We washed and painted the skateboards last month. _____

2. I shall know about the potatoes next week. _____

3. Potatoes were sold last week. _____

4. We know Mrs. Jones is wonderful. _____

5. Connie knows everything there is to know. _____

6. Cary deals cards properly. _____

7. Johnny took the three pigs to market. _____

8. Pigs are my favorite. _____

9. You will eat a wonderful meal at Kathy's place. _____

10. I am going crazy. _____

11. We shall sing in Mr. Aulinger's choir. _____

12. We do work for Mr. Jones. _____

13. Billy saw the big trucker yesterday. _____

14. You will try to behave in Mr. Wilson's room. _____

15. Molly was just thinking about the work. _____

16. I shall look cool. _____

17. Mr. Borycki, you are running late. _____

18. We have known Bighampton. _____

19. It remains to be seen. _____

20. I wrote the letter. _____

21. I'm choosing the teams. _____

22. She did write the love letter. _____

Name_____ Date_____

86. Using Capitals Properly

★ The sentences below do not have capitals. Cross out each small letter that should be a capital and write the capital letter above it. The first one is done for you.

    L   B   B

1. ~~l~~ast night ~~b~~ighampton saw ~~b~~reanna's car.

2. canada is a large and cold country with nice warm people.

3. mike saw jamalia at the johnson market on saturday.

4. bighampton took breanna to see *space cadets from venus* at the theatre.

5. sonia really liked bighampton in the school play.

6. breanna was jealous of this new girl from los alamos.

7. aunt kathy moved here from malta, montana.

8. cody, wyoming has a wonderful buffalo bill museum.

9. last week jamalia and mike went hiking on sugar mountain in yoho national park.

10. on saturday bighampton butler jones flew to boise with akira.

11. breanna works at the flamingo motel as a chambermaid after school on wednesdays.

12. miss bartel, the principal of alexander school, is going to poughkeepsie.

Copyright © 2002 by John Wiley & Sons, Inc.

Name_____ Date_____

87. Baseball Vowel Strikeout

★ Your task is to find the baseball words from the Choice Box below that are hidden in the puzzle.

★ All the vowels (A, E, I, O, U, Y) have been removed or "struck out." You will have to write the vowels in place as you find the words.

R	○	C	○	R	D	S	R	B	P	X	R	W	X	M	B	F	T
C	S	P	○	T	M	N	D	W	○	○	P	G	L	○	V	○	F
N	M	F	○	○	L	D	○	R	T	T	X	V	P	○	W	L	○
V	○	○	D	T	C	S	P	T	○	○	T	M	N	N	W	○	S
S	S	○	○	D	C	M	○	S	L	○	D	○	R	D	M	N	T
T	T	L	○	D	F	H	○	M	○	R	○	N	R	R	M	○	B
○	R	B	B	○	S	○	F	F	P	Q	P	W	○	M	D	○	
○	○	○	L	R	T	V	P	C	D	F	R	B	○	N	N	R	L
L	K	L	○	M	M	D	○	○	M	○	N	D	M	N	P	○	L
T	○	L	M	J	D	R	C	J	P	L	○	M	L	○	L	V	R
N	P	B	H	○	M	○	P	L	○	T	○	S	T	R	R	○	T
F	L	○	B	○	L	L	K	N	S	D	F	R	P	B	○	N	T

CHOICE BOX

base	fielder	home run	records
batter	fly ball	line drive	runner
bunt	foul ball	mound	safe
diamond	glove	out	slide
double	hitter	pitch	stadium
fastball	home plate	RBI	steal
			strike

Name_____ Date_____

88. Using and Understanding Suffixes

★ Here are groups of five words. Your job is to choose a word part called a *suffix* that will fit at the end of each word in order to make a completely new word.

★ All the words in the same group have the same suffix.

★ Suffixes to choose from are in the Suffix Box. Not all suffixes are used.

★ Write the correct suffix on the line next to the given word. The first group has been done for you.

SUFFIX BOX

able	ish	less	ful	ance	ate	ed	ive	ty
ness	y	ing	ment	tion	en	ous	ity	

1. play _ed_   work _ed_   display _ed_   hush _ed_   hunt _ed_

2. treat _____   live _____   color _____   reason _____   remark _____

3. wonder _____   help _____   hope _____   play _____   thank _____

4. power _____   hope _____   pain _____   care _____   use _____

5. fool _____   self _____   fiend _____   fever _____   child _____

6. sport _____   jaunt _____   fault _____   curl _____   filth _____

7. abate _____   refresh _____   pronounce _____   abandon _____   enjoy _____

8. drunk _____   height _____   less _____   soft _____   hard _____

9. combat _____   destruct _____   correct _____   object _____   select _____

10. fly _____   hold _____   fight _____   think _____   feel _____

95

89. Using and Understanding Prefixes

★ Here are groups of five words. Your job is to choose a word part called a *prefix* that will fit at the beginning of each word in order to make a completely new word.

★ All words in the same group have the same prefix.

★ Prefixes to choose from are in the Prefix Box. Not all prefixes are used.

★ Write the correct prefix on the line in front of the given word. The first group has been done for you.

PREFIX BOX

pro	re	ad	sub	un
any	ex	in	com	mis
trans	dis	anti	de	inter

1. _un_ happy   _un_ couth   _un_ tied   _un_ done   _un_ couple

2. _____ turn   _____ place   _____ tired   _____ moved   _____ built

3. _____ come   _____ justice   _____ land   _____ operable   _____ organic

4. _____ social   _____ freeze   _____ ballistic   _____ body   _____ climax

5. _____ time   _____ place   _____ one   _____ thing   _____ way

6. _____ fine   _____ file   _____ throne   _____ humidify   _____ fame

7. _____ figure   _____ fix   _____ action   _____ Atlantic   _____ scribe

8. _____ place   _____ name   _____ fortune   _____ giving   _____ lead

9. _____ change   _____ lock   _____ collegiate   _____ continental   _____ galactic

10. _____ act   _____ tradition   _____ change   _____ claim   _____ traction

Name _____ Date _____

90. Thou Shalt Enjoy This Vowelless Puzzle

★ Henceforth thou are to find the correct "Pilgrims of Plymouth Colony" words hidden in the puzzle. The word list is given below in the Choice Box.

★ All the vowels (A, E, I, O, U, Y) have been removed.

★ You will need to write the vowels in place as you find the words.

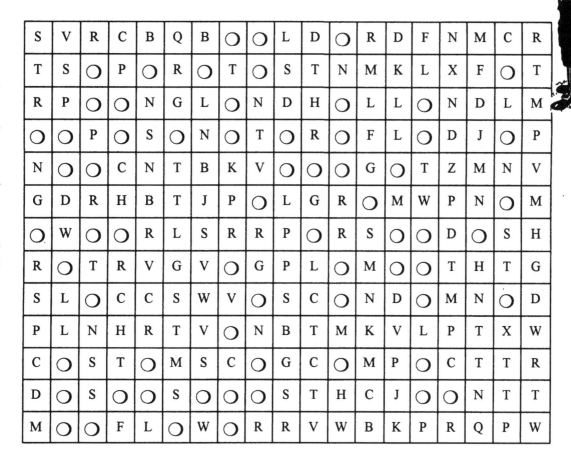

S	V	R	C	B	Q	B	○	○	L	D	○	R	D	F	N	M	C	R
T	S	○	P	○	R	○	T	○	S	T	N	M	K	L	X	F	○	T
R	P	○	○	N	G	L	○	N	D	H	○	L	L	○	N	D	L	M
○	○	P	○	S	○	N	○	T	○	R	○	F	L	○	D	J	○	P
N	○	○	C	N	T	B	K	V	○	○	○	G	○	T	Z	M	N	V
G	D	R	H	B	T	J	P	○	L	G	R	○	M	W	P	N	○	M
○	W	○	○	R	L	S	R	R	P	○	R	S	○	○	D	○	S	H
R	○	T	R	V	G	V	○	G	P	L	○	M	○	○	T	H	T	G
S	L	○	C	C	S	W	V	○	S	C	○	N	D	○	M	N	○	D
P	L	N	H	R	T	V	○	N	B	T	M	K	V	L	P	T	X	W
C	○	S	T	○	M	S	C	○	G	C	○	M	P	○	C	T	T	R
D	○	S	○	○	S	○	○	○	S	T	H	C	J	○	○	N	T	T
M	○	○	F	L	○	W	○	R	R	V	W	B	K	P	R	Q	P	W

CHOICE BOX

boulder	customs	joint	privacy	Speedwell
church	disease	Mayflower	Puritan	stock
Colonist	England	persuade	Saints	strangers
compact	fled	Pilgrim	sanitary	Virginia
condemned	Holland	Plymouth	Separatist	voyage

SECTION 4

SUCCESS

LEARNING

LEARNING

ESSENTIAL STRATEGIES FOR LANGUAGE DEVELOPMENT

91. Finding Words from Clues and Scrambles

★ The descriptions in Column 1 are clues to finding the word you need for Column 2.

★ Column 2 is the word you need for Column 3; however, it is scrambled.

★ Write the circled letters from Column 3 in order at the bottom of the page to reveal a true fact about you and your classmates. The first one is done for you.

	COLUMN 1—CLUES	COLUMN 2	COLUMN 3
1.	to question someone	k a s	_ (S) _
2.	a very conceited person	r o a n g r a t	_ _ _ _ _ _ _ O
3.	to attack someone	s a l t u s a	_ _ _ _ O _ _
4.	the name or label on a product	r d a b n	_ _ _ _ O
5.	shameless or bold	a n z b r e	_ _ _ _ O _
6.	to make wide	o d e b r a n	_ _ _ _ _ _ O
7.	something or someone very delicate	i d t n a y	_ _ _ _ O _
8.	old-fashioned name for girl/maiden	a s l d m e	_ _ _ O _ _
9.	an Old West name for a bandit	e p r d d s e a o	_ _ _ _ _ _ O _ _
10.	the membrane in the ear	a d u m r r e	_ _ O _ _ _ _
11.	to shrink or make less	d i d e l n w	_ _ _ _ _ _ O
12.	to spend money wildly	x r a g a n t t v e a	_ _ _ _ _ O _ _ _ _ _
13.	a chicken	n e h	_ O _
14.	to err or totter	a t r e l f	_ _ _ _ _ O
15.	a daydream	n a s t f a y	_ _ _ _ _ _ O
16.	a tall tale or a lie	a r c h f e t e d f	_ _ _ _ _ _ O _ _ _
17.	in the public eye, well known	m o s u a f	_ _ _ O _ _
18.	leaves, twigs	l a e f o i g	_ O _ _ _ _ _
19.	a laughable, amusing situation	i a i u s h l r o	_ _ O _ _ _ _ _

S _____

Name _____ Date _____

92. Building a Limerick

Quick Access Information ➔ A limerick is an amusing five-line poem in which lines one, two, and five rhyme, and lines three and four rhyme.

★ Your task is to read the first limerick which is complete. You then add your own last line to number 2, two lines to number 3, and so on until you finally write your own complete limerick for number 6.

1. There was a young ghost called Doreen
   Whose name wasn't scary or mean.
   She changed it to Boo
   And now it is true,
   She's frightened by herself on Halloween.

2. There was a young ghost called Doreen
   Whose name wasn't scary or mean.
   She changed it to Boo
   And now it is true,

   _____

3. There was a young ghost called Doreen
   Whose name wasn't scary or mean.
   She changed it to Boo

   _____

   _____

4. There was a young ghost called Doreen
   Whose name wasn't scary or mean.

   _____

   _____

   _____

5. There was a young ghost called Doreen

   _____

   _____

   _____

   _____

6. _____

   _____

   _____

   _____

   _____

BOO

93. Understanding Double Negatives

Quick Access Information ➔ Following are a number of sentences that use double negatives. They, in effect, say the opposite of what the speaker really wants to say. Double negatives are often combined with other forms of poor English.

★ **Rewrite these double negatives in proper sentence form using only one negative and correct English grammar.**

1. "I never have no fun," said Figgy.

   _____

2. I don't have none of those green elephants.

   _____

3. I haven't hardly started my essay.

   _____

4. I can't find nothing to do.

   _____

5. I haven't never had such a rare steak.

   _____

6. I don't gots none nohow.

   _____

7. Don't you never have such a horse as that?

   _____

8. Elephants aren't never small.

   _____

9. She wasn't nowhere today.

   _____

10. Joe hasn't never landed a space shuttle.

    _____

94. Placing Words in Context

★ The words in the Choice Box are to be used in the story below in order to make it complete.

★ Cross out each word after you have placed it in its correct location.

Benny Smith was a very _____ young man. He never had any _____ for candy or other goodies that he so much desired. His mother was a _____ parent who worked at two jobs just to make _____ meet.

Benny had to look after himself and his little _____ after school. Some people called him a _____ kid. This didn't bother Benny because he had a _____. He was going to play _____ when he grew up. Already he was able to play with the high school students in the yard behind the _____ even though he was _____.

Benny knew he had to work hard to break the cycle of _____. One thing he knew to do was to eat the _____ foods. If he was to _____ tall enough, he had to have the proper _____. His mom made every _____ to feed Benny and his eight-year-old sister _____.

One day Benny saw that he was a _____ player than the best high school _____. With more hard _____ and proper eating habits, Benny _____ to be seven feet two inches by the time he finished high school. _____ league scouts were all after him to sign a contract.

His _____ life made the difference. Now, Benny is a top player in the _____ and a fine example to all kids who have to do it the _____ way.

CHOICE BOX

basketball	effort	hard	NBA	properly	student
better	ends	latchkey	nutrition	right	tenement
clean	grew	major	poor	single	thirteen
dream	grow	money	poverty	sister	work

95. Using Words Correctly

★ **At the end of each sentence are two or more words. Circle the correct word or phrase that completes each sentence.**

1. The teens and adults _____ had a great time. (**sure, surely**)

2. Mr. Poulin said they had _____ excellent French words. (**wrote, written**)

3. *The Way of the Samurai* is _____ great also. (**real, really**)

4. The cats almost _____ themselves out by fighting. (**wore, worn**)

5. "_____ video, *Bandits Lose,* is the best," said Sunshine. (**This, Thus, This here**)

6. No one would _____ Mortal Kumquat off the list. (**leave, let**)

7. Bighampton's essay had _____ everyone away. (**drive, drove, driven**)

8. "_____ me have it this week," Jason demanded. (**Let, Leave**)

9. Do you remember Bighampton _____ *The Space Cadets*? (**write, written, writing**)

10. That dark evening Bighampton _____ home on his BMX. (**rode, ridden, ride**)

11. I think *Buster Blaster* is _____ exciting video. (**a, an**)

12. "I know Bighampton has _____ the world's greatest essay," said Breanna. (**wrote, written**)

13. Of course _____ video games have the best graphics! (**these, those, these here**)

14. _____ video games with colorful graphics are outstanding. (**Them, Those**)

15. "_____ videos were very expensive," said Breanna. (**These, Them**)

96. The Language Enrichment Chart

★ Below is a chart that will have 45 words. Your task is to choose three words from the Choice Box that relate or have something to do with each clue. Cross out each word after you use it.

	CLUES	RELATED WORDS		
1.	videos			
2.	school			
3.	eating			
4.	noise			
5.	running			
6.	love			
7.	littleness			
8.	vehicle			
9.	bigness			
10.	angels			
11.	anger			
12.	seeing			
13.	things to open			
14.	movement			
15.	people			

CHOICE BOX

action	echo	gobble	loud	scurry
affection	electronic	heavenly	mad	sight
appetite	enormous	homework	mankind	small
archangel	flight	huge	observe	tiny
bang	flow	humanity	peewee	travel
books	fondness	hungry	person	truck
car	gallop	irk	race	view
cherub	games	large	rage	wagon
door	gate	liking	ruler	window

97. Using Distinctive or Character Words in Context

★ Some words are full of character and strength and therefore carry a lot of meaning. That meaning is best shown when the words are used as part of a sentence or paragraph. This is called "in context." They enrich the writing without changing the story.

★ Rewrite the paragraph on the lines below and choose the distinctive words from the Choice Box to replace the underlined words or phrases. Not all words in the Choice Box will be used. (Use another sheet of paper if you need more space.)

Once upon a time there were three <u>okay</u> little pigs. They were very <u>happy</u> until a local <u>bad</u> wolf with attitude came looking for food. The wolf gave them <u>an ill feeling</u>, so they decided to <u>run</u> because he appeared <u>harmful</u>. This was a sudden <u>shock</u> to the pigs' <u>wonderful</u> lifestyle. The pigs <u>thought</u> for a moment and said, "Let's stay and <u>win</u> against this <u>large</u> force because we are <u>active</u> and have <u>strength</u>. We will not be afraid of this <u>bad animal</u>." By using their intelligence, the pigs tricked the wolf into falling into a <u>pot</u> of hot water. The wolf ran away, never to be seen again. The pigs returned to their lifestyle and lived without <u>feeling bad about it</u> ever after.

_____

_____

_____

_____

_____

_____

_____

_____

_____

CHOICE BOX

agile	dilapidated	jolly	nimble	regret	shifty
beast	energy	jolt	ogre	remorse	strong
cauldron	fantastic	marvelous	overbearing	rumble	triumph
contemplated	glorious	nasty	overpowering	scamper	troll
destroy	jitters	nifty	power	shakes	vibrant

98. Alphabetizing

★ Find the word in each list that is not in alphabetical order. Rewrite the list correctly on the line below.

1. promote, prompt, proof, prone, prop, proper

_____

2. rock, rod, rogue, roll, romp, romance

_____

3. suffix, suggest, sugar, suit, sulk, summit

_____

4. approve, aquatic, arbor, arch, arise, arena

_____

5. crest, creep, crew, crime, crisis, crooked

_____

6. rise, rival, risk, river, road, roast

_____

7. shout, shot, show, shrewd, shrine, shrivel

_____

8. too, top, torch, topic, toss, total

_____

9. vacant, vacate, vacation, vague, vagabond, vain

_____

10. zany, zealot, zeal, zenith, zero, zest

_____

Name_____ Date_____

99. Alphabetical Sports and Activities

★ There are 24 words hidden in the letters below. The words name sports and activities students can do at school.

★ Find each word and put it in alphabetical order on the lines provided. Be careful! The words can be broken and continue on the next line.

volleyballfootballbadmint
ontennisshotputbandswim
mingtrackjavelincheerlead
inggymnasticsskippingice
hockeytabletenniscamerac
lubdebatingtiddlywinkshig
hjumporatorydramawrestli
ngweightliftingbasketballb
iblestudy

1. _____   9. _____   17. _____

2. _____   10. _____   18. _____

3. _____   11. _____   19. _____

4. _____   12. _____   20. _____

5. _____   13. _____   21. _____

6. _____   14. _____   22. _____

7. _____   15. _____   23. _____

8. _____   16. _____   24. _____

100. Organizing by Alphabetizing

★ When you work in an office, you need to know the alphabet very well in order to file papers and other things in their proper place.

1. Sort the stack of folders into two groups. Stack 1 is for folders of people whose last names begin with any letter from <u>A to K</u>. Stack 2 is for people whose last names begin with <u>L to Z</u>. Next to each name listed below, place the number of the stack (1 or 2) in which it belongs.

____ Kallback	____ Hall	____ Poulin
____ Tilford	____ Heffernan	____ Robinson
____ Anthony	____ Johnson	____ Tegart
____ Aulinger	____ Lengyel	____ Waldner
____ Zizmarthy	____ Oke	____ Elgert
____ Brenna	____ Parent	____ Stade

2. You must now arrange some other folders in alphabetical order. You can do this by numbering the names from 1 to 9 to show the correct order.

____ Wilson	____ Carpentier	____ Dament
____ Smith	____ Ruberry	____ McCallum
____ Bighampton	____ King	____ Moir

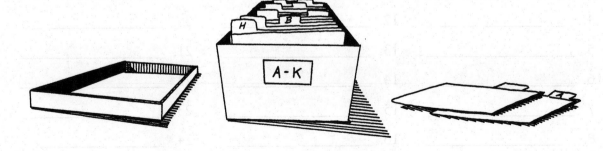

Name _____ Date _____

101. Lazy Language Puzzle

★ Many words and phrases are run together to make a statement. While it may be convenient or may even become a popular saying, it is not the proper way to speak.

★ Listed below are 15 run-together expressions. Circle the correct way to say each one in the puzzle below. One is completed for you.

1. woncha
2. wassup
3. wudja
4. lemme
5. gotcha

6. comere
7. cancha
8. gimme
9. Idunno
10. wannabe

11. hafta
12. howarya
13. didju
14. gedout
15. gotta

W	B	C	A	N	T	Y	O	U	R	E	D	S	T	E
A	W	J	I	W	D	I	D	Y	O	U	B	M	N	I
N	O	W	O	N	T	Y	O	U	P	N	R	W	S	U
T	U	R	V	Y	P	C	C	O	M	E	H	E	R	E
T	L	D	S	V	I	H	V	B	N	J	A	O	K	L
O	D	W	R	E	G	O	T	T	O	U	V	M	T	G
B	Y	B	N	I	E	I	L	E	T	M	E	M	U	O
E	O	P	V	U	T	D	U	N	B	U	T	I	L	T
G	U	E	C	H	O	W	A	R	E	Y	O	U	T	Y
H	M	I	U	S	U	D	W	H	A	T	S	U	P	O
E	I	D	O	N	T	K	N	O	W	V	W	R	T	U

102. Spelling Civil War Battles: Part One

★ The names of two U.S. Civil War battles have been mixed together above each puzzle.

★ Your task is to unscramble the letters in order to spell the names of the battles in the spaces below. The names can be found in the Battle List.

★ One name has been given to help you get started.

K H N T Y T O A F C A R K N A N O G L   H T I T S Y B H R L G U O G E

–   _ _ _ _ _ _ _ _ _ _
–   –
–   –
–   –
F R A N K L I N   –
–
–
–
–

R K B P E R B U I V S T U G E R C G   O E T Y E A R P I V S S V P A R N I L L L

–   –
–   –
_ _ _ _ _ _ _ _ _ _   _ _ _ _ _ _ _ _ _ _ _ _
–   –
–   –
–   –

BATTLE LIST

Chattanooga	Franklin
Gettysburg	Perryville
Petersburg	Shiloh
Spotsylvania	Vicksburg

Name_____ Date_____

103. Spelling Civil War Battles: Part Two

★ The names of two U.S. Civil War battles have been mixed together above each puzzle.

★ Your task is to unscramble the letters in order to spell the names of the battles in the spaces below. The names can be found in the Battle List.

V S L U U L R C H R B A L L E N N C E O I L

K F D U A R G U H S R I E C E K R B C C A M G A

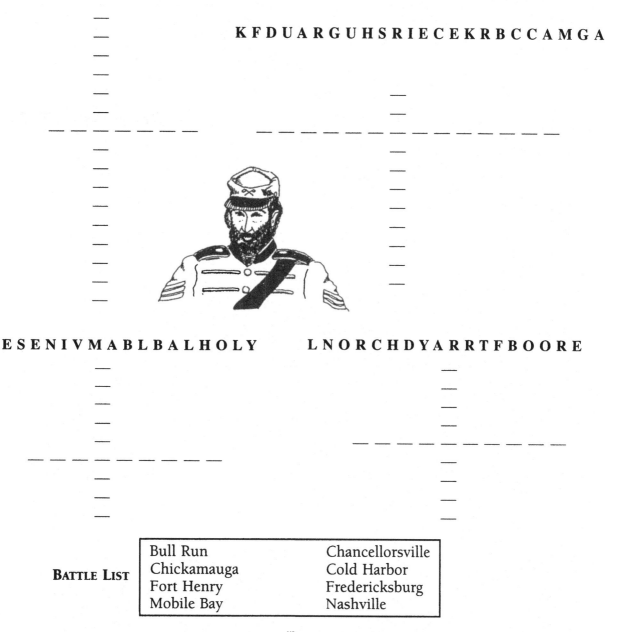

E S E N I V M A B L B A L H O L Y   **L N O R C H D Y A R R T F B O O R E**

BATTLE LIST

Bull Run	Chancellorsville
Chickamauga	Cold Harbor
Fort Henry	Fredericksburg
Mobile Bay	Nashville

104. Titanic Words and Expressions

★ Some words are more well known today because they somehow were associated with the ill-fated *Titanic*.

★ Match the word or expression from the Choice Box with the correct meaning of that word.

1. These are the compartments that were supposed to keep water from flooding into the *Titanic*. _____

2. This ship rescued 705 passengers from lifeboats. _____

3. These held the lifeboats in place onboard ship. _____

4. A large floating body of ice is called an _____.

5. This was the rumor about the *Titanic* that proved to be untrue.
_____

6. The weight of a ship is described in this term. _____

7. The first voyage of a ship or airplane is called its _____.

8. The company that built the *Titanic* was called the _____.

9. _____ is the name of the port the *Titanic* sailed from in Europe.

10. This expression was used to describe what groups of people were saved first.
_____

11. The captain's control center is called _____.

12. This word means strong, large, and mighty. _____

13. This device helps people float in the water. _____

14. This is the area of the ship where the immigrants traveled while on the *Titanic*.
_____

15. This number of smokestacks is now considered unlucky by sailors and shipbuilders.
_____

Copyright © 2002 by John Wiley & Sons, Inc.

CHOICE BOX

<u>Carpathia</u>	life jacket	the bridge	water-tight
davits	maiden voyage	Titan	compartments
four	Southampton	tonnage	White Star Line
iceberg	steerage	unsinkable	women and children first

105. Vocabulary Development with President Lincoln

★ Use only the letters in the name ABRAHAM LINCOLN to form words that answer the clues.

★ Letters are used more than once in some words.

1. A place to store grain is a ___ ___ ___.

2. A person who does not tell the truth is a ___ ___ ___ ___.

3. You fill a cup to the ___ ___ ___ ___.

4. The usual name of the center street in a town is ___ ___ ___ ___.

5. The gray matter in your head is your ___ ___ ___ ___ ___.

6. A place where experiments are conducted is a ___ ___ ___.

7. The "king of beasts" is the ___ ___ ___ ___.

8. Not your papa but your ___ ___ ___ ___.

9. A Jewish religious leader is a ___ ___ ___ ___ ___.

10. Another name for the nickel in your pocket is a ___ ___ ___ ___.

11. A snake found in India or the name of a 1960s sports car is a ___ ___ ___ ___ ___.

12. The month after February is ___ ___ ___ ___ ___.

13. You put this around a gift: a ___ ___ ___ ___ ___ ___.

14. A long yellow fruit with a slippery peel is a ___ ___ ___ ___ ___ ___.

15. White ice particles that fall in the summer are ___ ___ ___ ___.

16. A place where there are many stores is a ___ ___ ___ ___.

17. A place where cows are milked is a ___ ___ ___ ___.

18. Jack and Jill went up this to fetch a pail of water: the ___ ___ ___ ___.

19. This is called an "ear" and is yellow: ___ ___ ___ ___.

20. You have this on top of your head: ___ ___ ___ ___.

21. When you are the most popular kid in town, you are said to be ___ ___ ___ ___.

22. The opposite of her is ___ ___ ___.

23. The short way of saying limousine is to say ___ ___ ___ ___.

24. A male sheep is a ___ ___ ___.

25. The opposite of excited is ___ ___ ___ ___.

Name_____ Date_____

106. "F"-Sounding Words with No "F"

★ Find words in the Choice Box that have the "F" sound that suit or fit each definition.

★ The "F" sound could be anywhere in the word.

1. _____ You talk on this for hours on end if you are a teenager.

2. _____ This was the forerunner of tapes and CD's.

3. _____ You could be an aunt or an uncle of this male.

4. _____ The old name for the kings of Egypt.

5. _____ This is a picture of you.

6. _____ This is the surface of the road when it is bumpy.

7. _____ Thomas Edison used to tap Morse Code on this.

8. _____ You ask for this when you see a famous person.

9. _____ This is a person who has lost his or her parents.

10. _____ You have had this when you are full.

11. _____ A theory that the shape of the skull determines the mind and character of a person.

12. _____ A line diagram that shows rise and fall of circumstances, events, or production.

13. _____ This is how cells make sugars from carbon dioxide and water.

14. _____ This describes the human body.

15. _____ You often do this when you have a cold.

16. _____ This is when the vein in a leg becomes inflamed.

17. _____ A boy's name that rhymes with tulip.

18. _____ This is another name for a druggist or a person who prepares medicine.

19. _____ This person is strong and resilient in hard times.

20. _____ This is a morbid or unnatural fear of something.

CHOICE BOX

autograph	orphan	phobia	physique
cough	pharaoh	phonograph	rough
enough	pharmacist	photograph	telegraph
graph	Philip	photosynthesis	telephone
nephew	phlebitis	phrenology	tough

Name_____ Date_____

107. Strange and Unusual "A" Words

★ Using the Choice Box below, place the correct strange or unusual word beside its description. There are more words than descriptions. A dictionary will help.

1. This word means side by side. _____

2. A disease caused by abnormal activity of the pituitary gland. _____

3. To become muddled or confused. _____

4. A French word meaning goodbye. _____

5. The Greek god of the winds. _____

6. The lofty nest of an eagle. _____

7. The shield or breastplate used to protect the Greek god Zeus. _____

8. A statement written down and sworn to be true. _____

9. A Greek writer of fables. _____

10. To be eager, curious, or excited. _____

11. An officer in the military who is the assistant to a superior officer.

    _____

12. A sea fish related to the herring but not as tasty. _____

13. Attributing human qualities to so-called gods. _____

14. A person who defends an idea or belief. _____

15. To give a decision in a dispute. _____

16. Signs of success or a favorable situation. _____

17. A shrub bearing many colorful flowers. _____

18. Blue or skyblue, the clear blue color of the sky. _____

19. A total or partial loss of the ability to use and understand words.

    _____

20. The point most distant from the sun. _____

CHOICE BOX

aboriginal	aegis	aide-de-camp	aphelia
abreast	Aeolus	aigrette	apologist
acromegaly	aerie	alewife	arbitrate
Adam's apple	Aesop	animus	auspicious
addled	affidavit	anthropomorphic	azalea
adieu	agog	aphasia	azure

108. Strange and Unusual "H" Words

★ Using the Choice Box below, place the correct word beside its description. A dictionary will help.

1. A word used when doing trickery or magic. _____

2. A Scottish delicacy made from the heart, liver, and lungs of a sheep. It is mixed with oatmeal and suet, then boiled in the stomach of the animal. _____

3. A dealer in men's hats, shirts, and ties. _____

4. Something used too often. _____

5. A small saltwater fish shaped like an eel. _____

6. A stringed musical instrument like a piano. _____

7. A jellied meatloaf formed from parts of the head and feet of pigs. _____

8. Another name for white frost. _____

9. To be reckless or careless or to act wildly. _____

10. A bag with a long strap used by soldiers. _____

11. The sound made by a donkey. _____

12. Another name for a porcupine in North America. _____

13. A two-wheeled cab for two passengers pulled by a horse. _____

14. The study of reptiles. _____

15. A large barrel or cask holding from 50–120 gallons of a liquid. _____

16. An informal expression that means to talk or visit together. _____

17. Something that is worthless, like a lie. _____

18. Meaning to show surprise and contempt at the same time. _____

19. An informal expression describing confusion and disorder. _____

20. Hand-operated organ or street piano, usually turned by a wheel. _____

Copyright © 2002 by John Wiley & Sons, Inc.

CHOICE BOX

haberdasher	hansom	headcheese	hoarfrost	hogwash
hackneyed	harpsichord	hedgehog	hobnob	hoity-toity
hagfish	harum-scarum	heehaw	hocus-pocus	huggermugger
haggis	haversack	herpetology	hogshead	hurdy-gurdy

109. Strange and Unusual "M" Words

★ Using the Choice Box below, place the correct strange or unusual word beside its description. A dictionary will help.

M *DID YOU MISS ME BIGHAMPTON?* BIGHA PTON

1. A large tomb. _____

2. A thin soft layer of animal tissue. _____

3. A state of violent, aggressive, uncontrolled actions. _____

4. When a person feels overly important. _____

5. A sound made by a cat. _____

6. A pie topping often found on a lemon pie. _____

7. A mythical monster with the body of a bull and the head of a man (or vice versa).

   _____

8. This describes a pampered boy or man who is fussed over. _____

9. A tool with jaws that can be adjusted. _____

10. A sound made by a cow. _____

11. A mock court held at a school of law for practice purposes. _____

12. A boot worn by Inuit or Eskimos. _____

13. A sticky, gummy, glue-like substance. _____

14. A method of doing something, a pattern. _____

15. A salamander. _____

16. A French soldier who uses a musket-type gun. _____

17. A fragrant substance once used as a gift by an extremely wise person.

   _____

18. When things are just average or so-so. _____

19. A southern flower of white, pink, or purple. _____

20. Body armor made of small metal rings. _____

CHOICE BOX

magnolia	megalomania	Minotaur	monkey wrench	mud puppy
mail	membrane	modus	moo	mukluk
mausoleum	meow	operandi	moot court	musketeer
mayhem	meringue	mollycoddle	mucilage	myrrh
mediocre				

110. Strange and Unusual "W" Words

★ Using the Choice Box below, place the correct strange or unusual word beside its description. A dictionary will help.

1. A town in Belgium where Napoleon was defeated. _____

2. You are this if you are fond of making jokes. _____

3. A shrub or tree whose berries are covered with wax. _____

4. A small kangaroo. _____

5. This means to be cowardly or very unhealthy looking. _____

6. Bead made from shells used by Native Americans as money. _____

7. A plant from whose leaves blue dye is made. _____

8. A deer of North America featuring long slender antlers. _____

9. A good-for-nothing person. _____

10. A person without a home or friends. _____

11. Threads running from side to side across a fabric. _____

12. A light and shallow rowboat for river use. _____

13. A small wig worn on the head. _____

14. An African antelope. _____

15. The name of a ghost in Scotland. _____

16. A small sum of money donated happily by a poor person. _____

17. A valley or ravine through which a stream flows. _____

18. A pulling or lifting machine. _____

19. To look sad or unhappy. _____

20. A lumberman's trunk or chest. _____

CHOICE BOX

wadi	wampum	Waterloo	white-livered	windlass
waggish	wanigan	wax myrtle	widow's mite	woad
waif	wapiti	weft	wiglet	woebegone
wallaby	wastrel	wherry	wildebeest	wraith

Name _____ Date _____

III. U.S.A. Spelling Puzzle

★ Using the state names from the Choice Box below, fill in the puzzle. One letter has been given to help you get started.

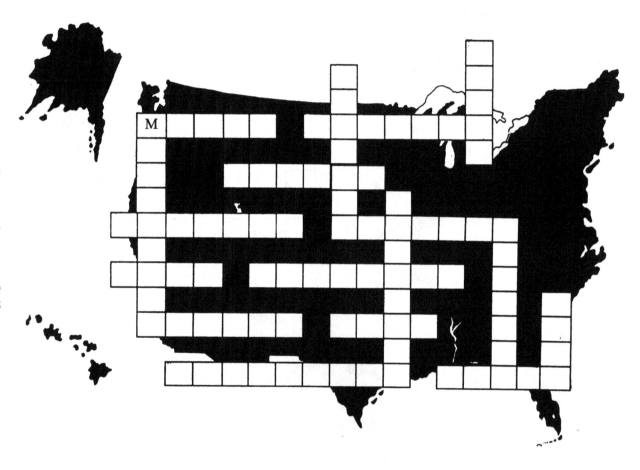

CHOICE BOX

Alabama	Hawaii	Minnesota	Oklahoma
Alaska	Idaho	Montana	Texas
Colorado	Iowa	New Mexico	Utah
Georgia	Maine	Ohio	Vermont
			Wyoming

112. World Spelling Puzzle

★ Using the country names from the Choice Box below, fill in the puzzle. One letter has been given to help you get started.

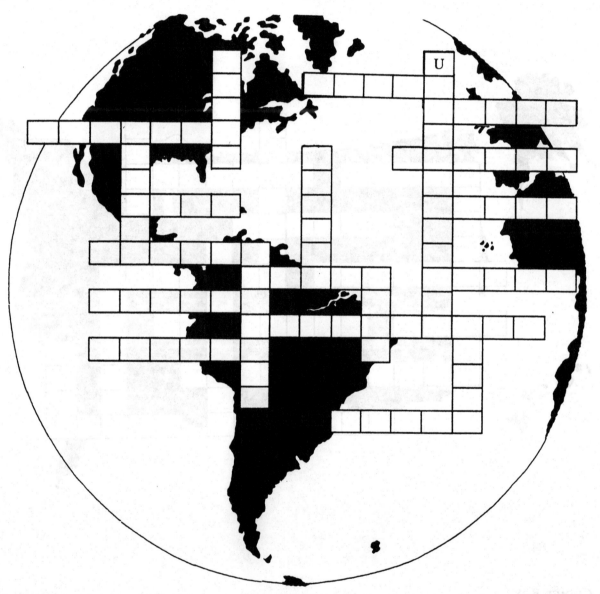

Copyright © 2002 by John Wiley & Sons, Inc.

CHOICE BOX

Belize	Egypt	Korea	Poland	Tibet
Canada	Germany	Libya	Spain	Togo
China	India	Madagascar	Sudan	Turkey
Denmark	Iran	Mexico	Sweden	United States

Name_____ Date_____

113. The Spelling Cube

★ Choose letters from the spelling cube to spell as many five-letter words as necessary to fill the chart.

★ A letter can be doubled or repeated if necessary.

★ Contractions and proper names are allowed.

★ Give yourself five points for each correct word.

★ One has been given to help you get started.

_____mouse_____   _____   _____

_____   _____   _____

_____   _____   _____

_____   _____   _____

_____   _____   _____

_____   _____   _____

_____   _____   _____

_____   _____   _____

_____   _____   _____

_____   _____   _____

_____   _____   _____

_____   _____   _____

_____   _____   _____

TOTAL POINTS _____

225

SECTION 5

THINKING AND REASONING SKILL BUILDERS

114. The Phobia Report: Part One

QUICK ACCESS
information

Quick Access Information ➜ A phobia has often been described as an abnormal or persistent fear about something in everyday life.

★   The Choice Box below lists ten phobias and the fear they each represent.

★   Choose a phobia to match each sentence.

WHAT DO YOU FEAR NOW?

BEING CAUGHT FOREVER ON A PHOBIA PAGE!

1. Molly said, "I'm afraid of this car because it is the thirteenth one I've owned."
_____

2. Molly blurted, "I can't stand the sight of blood, especially my own."
_____

3. Breanna fell down the stairs and now she fears them. _____

4. "I can't go to Canada," Bighampton said to me, "because they have this white cold stuff on the ground all winter." _____

5. "Who says no fear, I fear everything," Jamalia admitted. _____

6. Mike says, "I'm cool, except in a forest." _____

7. Breanna says she hates snakes. _____

8. "Get that cat away from me!" screamed Mike. _____

9. "I don't want the fur to touch me," he continued. _____

10. "I was scared to death at the edge of the Grand Canyon," Breanna admitted.
_____

CHOICE BOX

Ailurophobia—fear of cats	Hematophobia—fear of the sight of blood
Chionophobia—fear of snow	Hylophobia—fear of forests
Climacophobia—fear of stairs	Ophidiophobia—fear of reptiles
Cremnophobia—fear of precipices or edges	Pantrophobia—fear of everything
Doraphobia—fear of feeling or touching animal fur	Triskaidekaphobia—fear of the number 13

115. The Phobia Report: Part Two

> **Quick Access Information** ➔ A phobia has often been described as an abnormal or persistent fear about something in everyday life.

★ The Choice Box below lists ten phobias and the fear they each represent.

★ Choose a phobia to match each sentence.

1. Kate Johnson really dislikes large groups of people. _____

2. Gene Jo Aulinger ran from the wasp nest. _____

3. Molly Jones never wants to be joyous. _____

4. Breanna quit her job in the biology lab because of the germs.

   _____

5. "Get me off this bridge!" Bighampton yelled as he sweated.

   _____

6. "Get me out of this dwelling!" Bighampton yelled as he sweated.

   _____

7. "Stop worrying about the agony, suffering, hurt, ache, soreness, and discomfort, Mike. It's just a hangnail," Breanna revealed. _____

8. Mike blurted, "I am afraid to move." _____

9. "Don't leave me at the hospital all by myself," he cried. _____

10. "All the lights might be out in the waiting room," Mike said, as he rolled his eyes looking for sympathy. _____

CHOICE BOX

Achluophobia—fear of the dark	Kinesophobia—fear of motion
Bacillophobia—fear of microbes and bacteria	Melissophobia—fear of stinging insects
Cherophobia—fear of being happy	Monophobia—fear of being alone
Domatophobia—fear of being in a house	Ochlophobia—fear of crowds
Gephyrophobia—fear of crossing bridges	Odynophobia—fear of pain and agony

Name_____ Date _____

116. Working and Speaking Positively

★ The eighteen positive words listed in the Choice Box below are used in the story. Place the words where they belong. Some words are used more than once.

Jack and Jill were two _____ students at Beaumont Hill High School. They wanted to do something _____ that would fill their day with _____.

"Let's go fetch a pail of water," Jill said _____. "It will be _____," she continued.

"Big deal," Jack retorted, "look at my crown. I'm already king of our classroom. What could be more _____ than that? Besides, what's so great about a pail of water?"

"There's a big _____ for the person with the fullest pail of water."

"Sounds strange to me but for a serious _____ I will do it," he said in _____.

Soon Jack and Jill were advancing up Beaumont Hill. Jack kept looking around at the _____ view and adjusting the crown of which he was so _____.

"Come on, Jack," Jill _____. "We want to be the _____."

They soon _____ the hill and filled their pail with water.

Suddenly Jack yelled, "Oops."

All Jill could see was Jack tumbling end over end down Beaumont Hill. Frightened, Jill ran after him, still trying her _____ to carry her pail. _____ she did not spill a drop. She soon arrived at the bottom where Jack lay in a heap.

"How do you expect us to have _____ fortune and be a _____ if you keep abandoning me," she said sternly.

"Look at my _____ crown," Jack groaned, "it's broken to pieces. I thought you were supposed to come tumbling after me."

"I did give it some thought but saw no reason to do it," Jill replied, as she collected her winnings for having the _____ pail of water.

CHOICE BOX

anticipation	fantastic	pretty	success
best	fullest	prize	thrills
conquered	good	proud	winners
encouraged	happily	spectacular	wonderful
exciting	miraculously		

Name_____ Date_____

117. Mark Twain Quotes

★ Here are some famous quotes or sayings from one of America's favorite humorists. Each quote is described "in other words." Your task is to choose the correct quote from the Choice Box below and write it under the correct description of the quote.

1. My own habitual processes are perfect. It's other people who need to change their behavior.

_____

_____

2. Some people are saying I have passed away, but they are fibbing.

_____

_____

3. A black tabby won't live as long as an untruth.

_____

_____

4. In life it is better to have correct behavior because this will possibly help a person or two and totally amaze others.

_____

_____

5. When you are not sure of a situation, it is best to elicit honest behavior.

_____

_____

6. A well-spoken piece of reading material is often not indulged in.

_____

_____

CHOICE BOX

A. "Classic." A book which people praise and don't read.
B. The reports of my death are greatly exaggerated.
C. One of the most striking differences between a cat and a lie is that a cat has only nine lives.
D. Nothing so needs reforming as other people's habits.
E. When in doubt, tell the truth.
F. Always do right. This will gratify some people and astonish the rest.

118. Not the Same As . . .

★ Read each sentence below. Each one states that one thing is not the same as another. Your task is to explain how they are different.

1. Close is not the same as far because _____

_____

2. Meet is not the same as greet because _____

_____

3. Science is not the same as math because _____

_____

4. Lumpy is not the same as bumpy because _____

_____

5. Book is not the same as read because _____

_____

6. Machine is not the same as work because _____

_____

7. Love is not the same as like because _____

_____

8. Long is not the same as run because _____

_____

9. Tiger is not the same as lion because _____

_____

10. Quick is not the same as easy because _____

_____

119. Oxymorons Made Easy: Part One

> **Quick Access Information** ➔ An oxymoron is a group of words that have direct or implied contradictory (opposite) meanings that when used together make sense. If you say "awfully good," these words are opposite in meaning. How can something awful be good? Yet it still makes sense in the English language.

★ Listed below are eight underlined oxymorons. Your task is to tell how they are opposite in meaning and what their real meaning would be in context or the sentence.

1. The treasure <u>found missing</u> from the museum consisted of paintings.

   How words are opposite: _____

   Real meaning: _____

2. The <u>giant dwarf</u> star shone brightly.

   How words are opposite: _____

   Real meaning: _____

3. It was just <u>bad luck</u> that Molly did not win the lottery.

   How words are opposite: _____

   Real meaning: _____

4. <u>Jumbo shrimp</u> taste better than hamburger.

   How words are opposite: _____

   Real meaning: _____

5. Bighampton cleaned the <u>clogged drain</u> for his mother.

   How words are opposite: _____

   Real meaning: _____

6. A <u>lovers' quarrel</u> may lead to a breakup.

   How words are opposite: _____

   Real meaning: _____

7. Breanna threw the <u>hard cushion</u> at the cat.

   How words are opposite: _____

   Real meaning: _____

8. Believe me, this is <u>true gossip</u> about Mr. Watson.

   How words are opposite: _____

   Real meaning: _____

Name_____ Date _____

120. Oxymorons Made Easy: Part Two

Quick Access Information ➔ An oxymoron is a group of words that have direct or implied contradictory (opposite) meanings that when used together make sense. If you say "good grief," these words are opposite in meaning. There is nothing good about grief, yet it still makes sense in the English language.

★ Listed below are eight underlined oxymorons. Your task is to tell how they are opposite in meaning and what their real meaning would be in context or the sentence.

1. Mike says my dog is <u>pretty ugly</u>. _____

   How words are opposite: _____

   Real meaning: _____

2. Space walkers want their equipment to be <u>fail safe</u> so they can survive.

   How words are opposite: _____

   Real meaning: _____

3. The <u>silent alarm</u> was not detected by the thieves.

   How words are opposite: _____

   Real meaning: _____

4. It's all the <u>same difference</u> to me whether I have a horse or not.

   How words are opposite: _____

   Real meaning: _____

5. This is a <u>working vacation</u> because we are gaining from it.

   How words are opposite: _____

   Real meaning: _____

6. The gardener needs <u>clean dirt</u> to plant the flowers.

   How words are opposite: _____

   Real meaning: _____

7. Mr. Watson has <u>cool flames</u> on his 1934 Ford street rod.

   How words are opposite: _____

   Real meaning: _____

8. That picture fools nearly everyone but it is a <u>real fake</u> according to the expert.

   How words are opposite: _____

   Real meaning: _____

121. Seeing Both Sides of a Rule

★ People have opinions or personal points of view on many topics. Often other people will have a different opinion than you on a topic because there are frequently two or more sides to every story. Look at the school rules below and see if you can see what is good and what is not so good about them.

1. **Do not chew gum in school.** *Good:* _____

_____

Not so good: _____

_____

2. **Do not fight on school property.** *Good:* _____

_____

Not so good: _____

_____

3. **Do not run in the halls.** *Good:* _____

_____

Not so good: _____

_____

4. **You must wear a school uniform.** *Good:* _____

_____

Not so good: _____

_____

5. **Do not carry backpacks or book bags to class.** *Good:* _____

_____

Not so good: _____

_____

122. Rhyming Ratios

★ **Fill in the blanks with words that rhyme with the underlined word. The first one is done for you.**

1. Dog is to <u>cat</u> as shoe is to _____ hat _____.

2. Up is to <u>down</u> as smile is to _____.

3. Together is to <u>cut</u> as open is to _____.

4. Pretty is to <u>mess</u> as hate is to _____.

5. Young is to <u>old</u> as scared is to _____.

6. Square is to <u>round</u> as lost is to _____.

7. Sky is to <u>earth</u> as death is to _____.

8. Go is to <u>come</u> as stop is to _____.

9. Peace is to <u>fear</u> as far is to _____.

10. Open is to <u>close</u> as toe is to _____.

11. Happy is to <u>sad</u> as good is to _____.

12. Diamond is to <u>cheap</u> as gallop is to _____.

13. Circle is to <u>square</u> as crowded is to _____.

14. Light is to <u>dark</u> as street is to _____.

15. Hurt is to <u>happy</u> as slow is to _____.

16. Messy is to <u>clean</u> as nice is to _____.

17. Smooth is to <u>rough</u> as weak is to _____.

18. Head is to <u>toe</u> as rip is to _____.

19. Fire is to <u>water</u> as son is to _____.

20. Fix is to <u>break</u> as give is to _____.

The relationship of the "is to" words is _____

_____

123. Finding Mistakes

★ **Find the mistake(s) in the following sentences and rewrite the sentences correctly on the lines provided.**

1. None of the boys got their homework dun.

   _____

2. Them boys needs a talking to.

   _____

3. Bighampton was the worstest.

   _____

4. Vinny set Gina downs after the cheerleading routine.

   _____

5. Bighampton seys he lost his eyedentification in a flud.

   _____

6. Them pigs was in their sty.

   _____

7. Vinny don't like no pigs.

   _____

8. Ideas were Vinny's weakness points.

   _____

9. Stuff is wrote up slowly.

   _____

10. Vinny is a pal of hisn.

    _____

11. Ist you from duh Sout.

    _____

12. She coulduv gone to the Sout toos.

    _____

124. Building a Quote Using Video-Game Words

★ Fill in the blanks to form words 1 to 23. Put the underlined letters from the numbered words into the corresponding numbers below to discover a saying by e e cummings.

★ All words have been taken from video games.

1. Hea__

2. Launc__

3. Rogu__

4. Zon__

5. Dre__m

6. __aider

7. Opponen__

8. __ammer

9. Meta__

10. Im__ge

11. Cl__tch

12. __aming

13. Cras__

14. __torm

15. Glad__ator

16. U__real

17. __orce

18. Contro__ler

19. T__urnament

20. __acky

21. Fortr__ss

22. __aven

23. Conque__t

QUOTE:

" __ __ __ __ __ __ __ __ __ __ __ __ __ __ __ __
  1 2 3   4 5 6 7 8   9 10 11 12 13 14 15 16

__ __ __ __ __ __ __ " by e e cummings
17 18 19 20 21 22 23

125. Correct Context Usage

★   A sentence in a story that does not belong is said to be "out of context."

★   Read the story below to find sentences that don't belong in the story.

★   Draw a line through those sentences that are "out of context."

Once upon a time there were two wonderful students named Hansel and Gretel. They had a day off from the Woodlands Middle School, so they decided to explore the forest nearby. Hansel was at the doctor the day of the school video-game tournament.

Both Hansel and Gretel enjoyed exploring the woods because they loved nature. Gretel's dad had a flat tire on his pickup truck. They could smell the pine and fir trees as they got near the forest. It was so inviting that they went deep into the forest. Hansel's dog "Nero" was taken to the vet on Wednesday. "Look at all the squirrels and chipmunks," Hansel blurted as he skipped down the forest path.

"I went to the skateboard park," replied Gretel.

"This is strange," they both cried at once when they saw a tasty candy-covered cottage in the forest.

"Welcome here," a friendly, but ugly, witch stated. "I went for a ride in my car," she said.

"I'll have a taste of your house," Hansel replied. They entered the candy house of the friendly, but ugly, witch. The witch then thrust them into her oven and cackled, "Ah, ha, perhaps after this they will not trust strangers."

Suddenly Hansel and Gretel burst from the oven and fled from the candy house and the forest.

Back in school, Hansel said to Gretel, "We should e-mail Uncle Gene."

Copyright © 2002 by John Wiley & Sons, Inc.

126. Using Sentences to Show Relationships

★ Many things in the physical environment that have similarities appear to be very different. Your task is to describe in a complete, proper sentence how feature <u>A</u> is somehow like or related to feature <u>B</u>.

1. (A) mountain   (B) hill

_____

_____

2. (A) stream   (B) river

_____

_____

3. (A) tree   (B) forest

_____

_____

4. (A) volcano   (B) earthquake

_____

_____

5. (A) map   (B) road

_____

_____

6. (A) climate   (B) weather

_____

_____

7. (A) distance   (B) direction

_____

_____

8. (A) longitude   (B) latitude

_____

_____

127. Scary Things: Part One

★ On line 1, describe what you think the word means.

★ On line 2, give the dictionary definition of the word.

1. Apparition   (1) _____

                 (2) _____

2. Boo   (1) _____

                 (2) _____

3. Demented   (1) _____

                 (2) _____

4. Eerie   (1) _____

                 (2) _____

5. Ghoul   (1) _____

                 (2) _____

6. Haunting   (1) _____

                 (2) _____

7. Fright   (1) _____

                 (2) _____

8. Werewolf   (1) _____

                 (2) _____

128. Scary Things: Part Two

★ On line 1, describe what you think the word means.

★ On line 2, give the dictionary definition of the word.

1. **Bizarre**   (1) _____

 (2) _____

2. **Devious**   (1) _____

 (2) _____

3. **Fear**   (1) _____

 (2) _____

4. **Goblin**   (1) _____

 (2) _____

5. **Gruesome**   (1) _____

 (2) _____

6. **Ghastly**   (1) _____

 (2) _____

7. **Grotesque**   (1) _____

 (2) _____

8. **Mummy**   (1) _____

 (2) _____

Name_____ Date_____

129. How One Thing Is Like Another: Part One

★ Many things in life have similarities, even though at first they may appear to be very different.

★ Your task is to describe in a complete, proper sentence how item __A__ is somehow like item __B__.

1. **(A)** cup **(B)** soda can

_____

_____

2. **(A)** horse **(B)** giraffe

_____

_____

3. **(A)** book **(B)** movie video

_____

_____

4. **(A)** airplane **(B)** Space Shuttle

_____

_____

5. **(A)** hot rod **(B)** family van

_____

_____

6. **(A)** goose **(B)** duck

_____

_____

7. **(A)** glue **(B)** your best friend

_____

_____

8. **(A)** touchdown **(B)** a slam dunk

_____

_____

130. How One Thing Is Like Another: Part Two

★ Many things in life have similarities, even though at first they may appear to be very different.

★ Your task is to describe in a complete, proper sentence how item <u>A</u> is somehow like item <u>B</u>.

1. **(A)** stagecoach **(B)** covered wagon

_____

_____

2. **(A)** flagpole **(B)** broom

_____

_____

3. **(A)** gate **(B)** door

_____

_____

4. **(A)** tire **(B)** doughnut

_____

_____

5. **(A)** key **(B)** password

_____

_____

6. **(A)** chalk **(B)** pencil

_____

_____

7. **(A)** container ship **(B)** train

_____

_____

8. **(A)** CD (compact disk) **(B)** cassette tape

_____

_____

131. How One Thing Is Different from Another: Part One

★   Many things in life have differences, even though they may be connected in some way.

★   Your task is to describe in a complete, proper sentence how the two items in each line differ.

1. mule, horse _____

_____

2. cantaloupe, strawberry _____

_____

3. dog, camel _____

_____

4. bowl, goblet _____

_____

5. exhaustion, running _____

_____

6. ship, boat _____

_____

7. bell, siren _____

_____

8. brain, stomach _____

_____

9. want, order _____

_____

10. combat, command _____

_____

Name_____ Date _____

132. How One Thing Is Different from Another: Part Two

★ Many things in life have differences, even though they may be connected in some way.

★ Your task is to describe in a complete, proper sentence how the two items in each line differ.

1. movie, ticket _____

_____

2. old, middle age _____

_____

3. speed limit, slow _____

_____

4. coffee, cola _____

_____

5. hunter, prey _____

_____

6. race, chase _____

_____

7. question, tell _____

_____

8. hat, umbrella _____

_____

9. reduce, even _____

_____

10. solid, slime _____

_____

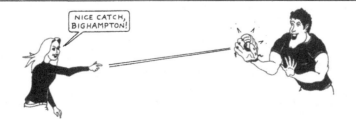

133. Brainstorming

★ Get into groups of not more than five, and have one brainstorming sheet for each group.

★ Discuss the central problem and come up with the most workable solution.

★ Here are the brainstorming rules:

 There are no wrong responses.
Try to come up with ten possible responses to help solve the problem.
No one is allowed to criticize someone else's response.
Try to arrive at the most workable answer to the problem.
Use responses from yourself and others to get better solutions.

Problem: **How to get a scared cat out of a tree**

1. _____
2. _____
3. _____
4. _____
5. _____
6. _____
7. _____
8. _____
9. _____
10. _____

Most workable solution: #____

Problem: **How to deal with the bully at school**

1. _____
2. _____
3. _____
4. _____
5. _____
6. _____
7. _____
8. _____
9. _____
10. _____

Most workable solution: #____

Copyright © 2002 by John Wiley & Sons, Inc.

134. Following Directions

★ Choose the most logical words from the boxes and put them into the sentences below. Words from Box A go with Sentence A. Words from Box B go with Sentence B, and so on. Some words will be used more than once.

A	B	C	D
chase, free spending, gold, produce, queen, venom	crowd, eternity, excellent, gorilla, gossip, haunt, musician	description, muddy, myth, nab, naval, promote	active, profit, ship, shiver, shock, tedious

1. **A.** The police will _____ the man with the _____.

   B. It is difficult for a _____ to _____.

   C. The _____ officer got _____ on the shore.

   D. People who own a _____ don't like it to be called a boat.

2. **A.** The _____ son wasted a lot of _____.

   B. It seemed like an _____ before the _____ started playing the violin.

   C. When the police had a _____ of the criminal, they were able to _____ her.

   D. When Darwin fell into the river, he was overcome with _____ and began to _____.

3. **A.** _____ Cleopatra died from the _____ of an asp.

   B. The _____ played for the _____ in an _____ way.

   C. The _____ captain said the story of "Blackbeard" was a _____.

   D. The stock market was _____ and everybody made a _____.

4. **A.** It is not easy to _____ a _____ scene in the movies.

   B. If you _____, your words may come back to _____ you.

   C. It was hard to _____ the bandit in the _____ water.

   D. The storekeeper was in _____ because of her massive _____.

Name_____ Date _____

135. Filling in the Verbs

★ The verbs (action words) have been removed from the following sentences. Your task is to fill each blank space with a suitable verb.

1. Karrie and Tony _____ to Bighampton's house.

2. They _____ to _____ his new dog.

3. Bighampton _____ a long leash to the animal.

4. The dog _____ very big.

5. Tony and Karrie _____ in wide-eyed disbelief.

6. The animal _____ across the field.

7. Bighampton's new dog _____ pointy ears, long hair on its tail, and _____, "Neigh."

8. Bighampton asked, "What do you _____ of my new German shepherd?"

9. Tony and Karrie had to _____ Bighampton that his new dog _____ actually a horse.

10. "Should I _____ him Rover or Fido?" Bighampton _____ as Tony and Karrie _____.

SECTION 6

PROBLEM SOLVING TO IMPROVE WORD USE AND UNDERSTANDING

136. What's the Time?

★   Here is a list of clues. Each clue describes a word or phrase that relates to time. Write your answer on the line.

1. The name of the time to come: _____

2. The name of the time that was: _____

3. The name of the time now: _____

4. The name of the day before today: _____

5. The name of the day after today: _____

6. 365 days equal one: _____

7. The number of months in a year: _____

8. The number of days in a week: _____

9. The number of hours in a day: _____

10. The name of a device for measuring time: _____

11. The number of terms a U.S. President can serve: _____

12. The number of days in a fortnight: _____

13. Your age in years and months: __ years __ months

14. Someone else's name and age in years and months: _____ (Name)
    __ years __ months

15. The number of days in a leap year: _____

16. The date of the leap year day: _____

17. Date summer holidays begin: _____

18. Your age to legally drive in your area: _____

19. Number of years in a decade: _____

20. Number of years in a century: _____

LOOKS LIKE TIME FLIES

Name_____ Date _____

137. Timelines

★ This timeline is designed to help you become aware of all you do in a school day. Fill in the details and how much time everything takes as you pass through each time period. List what you did, whom you talked to, where you went, and why you did things.

DAY OF THE WEEK _____

TIME PERIODS

7:00 A.M. _____

8:00 A.M. _____

9:00 A.M. _____

10:00 A.M. _____

11:00 A.M. _____

12:00 Noon _____

1:00 P.M. _____

2:00 P.M. _____

3:00 P.M. _____

4:00 P.M. _____

_____

Name_____ Date_____

138. Organizing Your Schedule

★ Everyone needs a schedule. If you don't have one, you may miss important events or appointments.

★ Help Sunshine and her twin sister, Moonbeam, with their schedule for the special week of exams, school meetings, and practices. Write in the name of activities where you think they belong in the schedule. The events and activities listed in the section are not in order.

★ One has been completed for you.

ACTIVITIES

Get out of bed, prepare, and walk to school—8 to 9 A.M., Daily
Math exam—9 to 11 A.M., Thursday
Science project meeting—1 to 3 P.M., Monday
Spare time at school—10 to 11 A.M., Friday and Tuesday
Student junior business meeting—9 A.M. to 12 Noon, Wednesday
Science exam—9 to 11 A.M., Monday
Sing in the school choir—1 to 3 P.M., Tuesday
Band practice—1 to 3 P.M., Friday
History essay writing—9 to 10 A.M., Friday
Lunch—12 Noon to 1 P.M., Daily
Volleyball practice—11 A.M. to 12 Noon, Monday, Tuesday, Thursday, Friday
Study time in library—9 to 10 A.M., Tuesday
Debating Club—1 to 3 P.M., Wednesday, Thursday

BIGHAMPTON-GET OFF THAT WORD. YOU'LL BREAK IT.

	MONDAY	TUESDAY	WEDNESDAY	THURSDAY	FRIDAY
8 A.M. 9 A.M.	Get out	of bed,	prepare, and	walk	to school
9 A.M. 10 A.M.					
10 A.M. 11 A.M.					
11 A.M. 12 NOON					
12 Noon 1 P.M.					
1 P.M. 2 P.M.					
2 P.M. 3 P.M.					

139. Understanding Shared Ideas/Concepts: Part One

★ Read the three words given on each line below. Think of what idea or concept they share or have in common. Write that idea/concept in the proper space beside each set of three words.

SHARED IDEA/CONCEPT

1. weary, fatigue, bore _____

2. twister, wind, storm _____

3. cavity, incisor, molar _____

4. red, green, blue _____

5. purchase, bargain, shop _____

6. painting, drawing, design _____

7. horse, monkey, dog _____

8. tires, hood, steering wheel _____

9. rock, tough, impenetrable _____

10. restrain, halt, hold _____

11. canine, paw, bark _____

12. phone, message, speaking _____

13. meow, whiskers, fur _____

14. marry, I do, gown _____

15. intelligence, brainy, bright _____

140. Understanding Shared Ideas/Concepts: Part Two

★ Read the three words given on each line below. Think of what idea or concept they share or have in common. Write that idea/concept in the proper space beside each set of three words.

SHARED IDEA/CONCEPT

1. boo, costume, October 31 _____

2. bat, ball, uniform _____

3. astronaut, shuttle, star _____

4. barn, cow, chicken _____

5. books, ruler, teacher _____

6. experiment, lab, beaker _____

7. money, mansions, fancy cars _____

8. clothes, beauty, elegance _____

9. virtual, fantasy, extreme _____

10. fortunate, joyous, ecstatic _____

11. bravery, valor, boldness _____

12. selection, pick, option _____

13. pass, kick, touchdown _____

14. hard drive, monitor, keyboard _____

15. abode, residence, dwelling _____

141. Understanding Shared Ideas/Concepts: Part Three

★ Read the three words given on each line below. Think of what idea or concept they share or have in common. Write that idea/concept in the proper space beside each set of three words.

SHARED IDEA/CONCEPT

1. powder, lipstick, mascara _____

2. shampoo, spray, mousse _____

3. receiver, friends, chatting _____

4. rings, earrings, necklace _____

5. sandals, pumps, sneakers _____

6. turtleneck, V-neck, pullover _____

7. tees, tops, blouse _____

8. candy bar, dark brown, milk _____

9. shorts, sundress, jumper _____

10. parka, mittens, boots _____

11. crafts, stamp collecting, woodworking _____

12. baseball, volleyball, badminton _____

13. doctor, truck driver, investment counselor _____

14. shoulder, clutch, hand _____

15. beret, tam, helmet _____

142. Getting Rid of Boring Verbs: Part One

★ Some sentences are just plain boring. That boredom usually comes from a lack-luster verb. Read the sentences below. Replace the underlined boring verb with an exciting or at least a more interesting one.

1. The pig <u>walked</u> into its pen. _____

2. The nice day <u>made</u> everyone happy. _____

3. My brother <u>looked</u> at the horse. _____

4. "Get away from the hot stove!" <u>said</u> Trevor. _____

5. "The girls <u>moved</u> toward me because I am cool," Bighampton said.

   _____

6. The huge diamond <u>went</u> for a high price. _____

7. The motorcycle gang <u>turned on</u> their engines. _____

8. The two Harleys <u>hit</u> each other. _____

9. "Let's go to the store," <u>said</u> Breanna. _____

10. Bighampton <u>put</u> holes in the paper. _____

11. The huge cat <u>came</u> onto her lap. _____

12. My older sister <u>sat</u> on the cactus. _____

13. Bree will <u>talk</u> with Bighampton. _____

14. Kangaroos can <u>hop</u> to the fence. _____

15. The tigers sat there ready to <u>move</u>. _____

BIGHAMPTON, ISN'T IT WONDERFUL TO BE WONDERFUL?

YES, IT IS, BREANNA. I DON'T KNOW WHAT WE WOULD DO IF WE WERE NOT SO WONDERFUL.

143. Getting Rid of Boring Verbs: Part Two

★ Some sentences are just plain boring. That boredom usually comes from a lack-luster verb. Read the sentences below. Replace the underlined boring verb with an exciting or at least a more interesting one.

THE ADVENTURES OF SHADOW THE CAT

1. Shadow was <u>wanting</u> some adventure. _____

2. She <u>came</u> into the bedroom. _____

3. She <u>saw</u> every corner of the room. _____

4. The lack of mice <u>troubled</u> her. _____

5. She <u>jumped</u> onto the bed. _____

6. Shadow <u>woke up</u> Karrie. _____

7. "You <u>are</u> such a pest," Karrie said. _____

8. Karrie <u>went</u> to the kitchen for cat food. _____

9. Shadow <u>walked</u> to the dresser. _____

10. Shadow <u>lay</u> down in the open drawer. _____

11. Karrie <u>returned</u> to the bedroom and <u>closed</u> the dresser drawer. _____,
_____

12. Karrie could not <u>find</u> Shadow to feed her. _____

13. Ten hours later Karrie <u>returned</u> from work and <u>looked</u> for Shadow.
_____, _____

14. Karrie could <u>hear</u> only a faint meow near the dresser. _____

15. Karrie, feeling bad, <u>rescued</u> the hungry, but well-rested Shadow.
_____

Name_____ Date _____

144. Emergency Response

★   Look at the Emergency Numbers below and answer the questions that follow.

SMALLER CENTERS		MOST CITIES
Emergency Numbers		**Dial 9-1-1**
Fire Department	555-4713	for:
Police	555-4848	Ambulance
Doctor	555-3278	Fire
Ambulance	555-6721	Police
Highway Patrol	555-4179	Highway Patrol
Travel Condition		
Hotline	555-2691	

1. Why is it a good idea to keep emergency numbers handy? _____

   _____

2. Most cities have the 9-1-1 emergency number. In a sentence, describe what help is

   available. _____

   _____

3. Smaller centers may not have the 9-1-1 emergency response system. In that case you

   should make your own list of emergency numbers. In a sentence, describe what ser-

   vices you should put on your list. _____

   _____

4. Why is there no doctor's name in the 9-1-1 list? _____

   _____

5. If you stub your toe and you live in a 9-1-1 response area, should you call the 9-1-1

   service? _____

   _____

6. What service do you think is provided by the Travel Condition Hotline? _____

   _____

Name_____ Date_____

145. Understanding Clichés and Idioms: Part One

> **Quick Access Information** ➡ We use idioms as a way of expressing ourselves. Usually they have a meaning other than the exact words expressed. A cliché is a time-worn expression that describes a thought.

★ The following is a list of eight idioms and clichés that have been rewritten in different words. Your task is to pick the correct idiom or cliché from the Choice Box and write its letter in the space provided.

1. Things that revolve in a circular fashion tend to reverse their direction and come back to the person who started it. ___

2. In the physical environment, the law of gravity dictates the vertical direction of entities or variables. ___

3. When a person uses a preventive measure in an early time frame, it often saves a numerical value of grief. ___

4. Co-exist. ___

5. The inscribing device has a stronger effect on the social structure than that which will be made into plowshares. ___

6. To be traveling by canoe northward in a small stream having lost one's propulsion device. ___

7. The chalice that he possesses seems to be overflowing. ___

8. This gentleman is a rather large social entity upon the hallowed halls of learning. ___

CHOICE BOX

A. His cup runneth over.	E. What goes up must come down.
B. He is a big man on campus.	F. A stitch in time saves nine.
C. What goes around comes around.	G. Live and let live.
D. Up the creek without a paddle.	H. The pen is mightier than the sword.

146. Understanding Clichés and Idioms: Part Two

Quick Access Information ➜ We use idioms as a way of expressing ourselves. Usually they have a meaning other than the exact words expressed. A cliché is a time-worn expression that describes a thought.

★ **The following is a list of eight idioms and clichés that have been rewritten in different words. Your task is to pick the correct idiom or cliché from the Choice Box and write its letter in the space provided.**

1. There may occur a situation when you cannot defeat an adversary, so your best bet is to form a liaison with that foe. ___

2. The person who deposits capital into the musician's coffers will say which song is to be played. ___

3. This person is developing the incorrect perspective on a problem. ___

4. This is an excellent way to make big bucks. ___

5. The perception of pulchritude lies within the paradigm of the perceiver. ___

6. One's apparel will heighten one's social status. ___

7. Great persons do not arrive in first place. ___

8. When something is finished on a good note, that thing is good. ___

CHOICE BOX

A. He is barking up the wrong tree.
B. Nice guys finish last.
C. All's well that ends well.
D. He who pays the piper calls the tune.
E. It's a license to print money.
F. If you can't beat them, join them.
G. Beauty is in the eyes of the beholder.
H. Clothes make the man (person).

147. Matching Idioms and Clichés to Their Meanings: Part One

> **Quick Access Information** ➡ Idioms are sayings people use to express themselves in conversation. They have another meaning other than what they actually say. A cliché is a time-worn expression that describes a thought.

★ **Your task is to match the idiom or cliché on the right with its correct meaning on the left.**

A. You are just like your parent.

B. To start some trouble.

C. Something is really good.

D. You have no idea or sense.

E. Slow down; don't be in such a hurry.

F. You are no fun.

G. You made a mistake.

H. The person does not listen.

I. You received the full penalty of the law.

J. It is useless or of no value.

K. You are nervous.

L. You bother me.

M. You took too much to eat.

N. Being dizzy from a hit.

O. You have an abundance of things.

P. Trying to act fancy.

Q. Leave this place.

R. To look with anger at someone.

S. In trouble (but not too serious).

T. To try to make someone feel sorry for you by crying large tears.

___ To cry crocodile tears.

___ Keep your shirt on.

___ In a pickle.

___ It is a white elephant.

___ Look daggers at.

___ To open a can of worms.

___ Far out.

___ Take a hike.

___ You are out to lunch.

___ You are a wet blanket.

___ You have butterflies in your stomach.

___ You laid an egg.

___ In one ear and out the other.

___ You get in my hair.

___ Your eyes are bigger than your stomach.

___ The judge threw the book at you.

___ Seeing stars.

___ Your cup runneth over.

___ Putting on the dog.

___ A chip off the old block.

148. Matching Idioms and Clichés to Their Meanings: Part Two

Quick Access Information ➡ Idioms are sayings people use to express themselves in conversation. They have another meaning other than what they actually say. A cliché is a time-worn expression that describes a thought.

★ **Your task is to match the idiom or cliché on the right with its correct meaning on the left.**

A. You said what I wanted to say.

B. Don't count on something before it comes to pass.

C. Things are going well for you right now.

D. Don't say the wrong thing.

E. Don't worry about something you can't do anything about.

F. Don't get angry so quickly.

G. You awoke in an angry mood.

H. Get to the point.

I. His boy acts like him.

J. Got the information from the source.

K. You are running from the police.

L. Ignore a problem.

M. To narrowly avoid a problem.

N. An expression used in the hippie days to mean something was "cool."

O. Do things in the proper order.

P. To ignore someone.

Q. Not a good idea or plan of action.

R. Tell me the truth.

S. You have a secret you keep hidden.

T. Don't reveal a secret.

___ Stop pulling my leg.

___ You have a skeleton in the closet.

___ Bury your head in the sand.

___ A close shave.

GROOVY! ___ Groovy.

___ Don't count your chickens before they hatch.

___ Don't put the cart before the horse.

___ You are sitting on top of the world.

___ Don't put your foot in your mouth.

___ Don't cry over spilled milk.

___ Don't let the cat out of the bag.

___ Don't fly off the handle.

___ You got up on the wrong side of the bed.

___ You took the words out of my mouth.

___ Don't beat around the bush.

___ Like father like son.

___ Give him/her the cold shoulder.

___ Straight from the horse's mouth.

___ You are on the lam.

___ Hare-brained scheme.

149. Presidential Match

★ Your task is to match the first names of some of the U.S. Presidents with their scrambled last names. Place the number of the last name on the line next to the President's first name.

Bill	___	1. N C U B H A A N
Woodrow	___	2. R H A T R U
James	___	3. A T E R C R
George	___	4. O H S N J N O
Calvin	___	5. Y D N E K N E
Lyndon	___	6. T T A F
Chester	___	7. E E R O F J F S N
William	___	8. V B R N N U E A
Ulysses	___	9. S I G T A W H N O N
Abraham	___	10. O L D G C O I E
Benjamin	___	11. I C L N L N O
Jimmy	___	12. A R I G D H N
Grover	___	13. L N T C I O N
John	___	14. O S V E T L R O E
Rutherford	___	15. Y R L T E
Millard	___	16. O D R F
John	___	17. L V E A C E L N D
Thomas	___	18. A A N R E G
Martin	___	19. O O E V E T R S L
Theodore	___	20. L S N W I O
Warren	___	21. O V R E H O
Ronald	___	22. L M R E F I L O
Gerald	___	23. A E Y H S
Franklin	___	24. A R S N H R I O
Herbert	___	25. R N T G A

150. Spelling Names of U.S. States and Presidents

★ Complete the names of these U.S. Presidents or states by answering the clues in parentheses.

★ Place the correct answer in the space provided.

1. _____more
   (pour into)

2. _____achusetts
   (church service)

3. North _____ina
   (female's name)

4. _____wa
   (debt)

5. _____ing
   (not soft)

6. _____idge
   (popular)

7. _____ Jersey
   (not old)

8. _____tucky
   (male's name)

9. _____ado
   (like paints)

10. Mon_____a
    (browning of skin)

11. _____er
    (wagon)

12. _____
    (shrub)

13. _____issippi
    (young girl)

14. _____ansas
    (Noah's boat)

15. _____inois
    (sick)

16. _____ington
    (to clean)

17. _____ho
    (female's name)

18. Cleve_____
    (ground)

19. Ruther_____
    (car company)

20. Oklaho_____
    (mother)

21. _____a
    (Native American)

22. _____hur
    (drawing)

23. _____ison
    (angry)

24. A_____s
    (holds water back)

151. Spelling U.S. Cities from Clues

★ Your task is to complete the names of the U.S. cities by using the clues in the parentheses. You may have to change the spelling slightly to spell the city name correctly in some cases.

1. _____a _____a, WA
(room side) (room side)

2. _____burg, OR
(flower)

3. _____apolis, IN
(Native American)

4. _____ison, WI
(angry)

5. _____ton, OH
(opposite of night)

6. Los _____es, CA
(heavenly body)

7. _____son City, NV
(automobile)

8. _____ Lake City, UT
(not sugar)

9. _____low, AZ
(not loses)

10. _____ Beach, CA
(not short)

11. Nor_____, VA
(persons)

12. Cleve_____, OH
(ground)

13. _____ville, KY
(a King of France)

14. Memp_____, TN
(male pronoun)

15. Bos_____, MA
(heavy weight)

16. Balti_____, MD
(not less)

17. Bing_____ton, NY
(pork)

18. Grand _____, ND
(eating utensils)

19. _____ing _____, KY
(alley sport)   (a color)

20. _____burgh, PA
(cherry centers)

21. Ros_____, NM
(deep hole)

22. Tam_____, FL
(dad)

23. New Or_____s, LA
(slim)

24. Little _____, AR
(stone)

25. _____ Rapids, MI
(large)

26. Oma_____, NE
(laugh)

27. _____ver, CO
(rec room)

28. New _____, CT
(safe area)

29. _____vidence, RI
(expert)

30. _____ado Springs, CO
(pigment)

31. _____sfield, CA
(bread chef)

32. Re_____, NV
(not yes)

33. _____haven, MS
(small stream)

34. _____immee, FL
(smooch)

35. _____ile, AL
(crowd)

36. Fort _____, TX
(of value)

152. What Would You Do If . . . : Part One

★   Write a full sentence to answer each of these unusual questions.

WHAT WOULD YOU DO IF:

1. Your favorite television star arrives at school and asks you to appear in an episode?

    _____

    _____

2. You throw some beans out your classroom window and suddenly they grow into a monstrous vine reaching high into the sky?

    _____

    _____

3. You are Cinderella and, after the charming prince put the glass slipper on your foot, you kiss him and he turns into a frog?

    _____

    _____

4. You win the Mega lottery but in order to get the money, you have to answer a question in math, a subject you dislike?

    _____

    _____

5. You are made "teacher for a day"?

    _____

    _____

6. You are Goldilocks and you are allergic to bear fur?

    _____

    _____

7. You arrive home from school one day to find it is 25 years in the past? Your friends are not born yet and your parents look like teenagers.

    _____

    _____

153. What Would You Do If...: Part Two

★   Write a full sentence to answer each of these not-so-unusual common life problems.

WHAT WOULD YOU DO IF:

1. Bighampton rises from your supper table and burps?

_____

_____

2. Bighampton argues, "To burp after a meal in some cultures is a sign of appreciation"?

_____

_____

3. Breanna walks into your house with muddy shoes?

_____

_____

4. Breanna insists that Bighampton open every door for her?

_____

_____

5. Akira goes to his aunt's wedding and fails to take off his baseball cap in church?

_____

_____

6. Some students are mocking Jamalia because she is in a wheelchair?

_____

_____

7. Bighampton comes to you for advice on how to break up with Breanna?

_____

Copyright © 2002 by John Wiley & Sons, Inc.

154. The People Puzzle

★ **Read the relationships below and then answer the questions. There may be more than one answer to each question.**

- Kathy is Tony's mother.
- Tony is Karrie's husband.
- George is Tony's father.
- Jack is Kathy's brother.
- Henry is Kathy's father.
- Maria is Kathy's mother.
- Ben is Frieda's husband.
- Maria is Ben's mother-in-law.

- Ruth is David's wife.
- Kevin is Ruth's son.
- Olaf and Eva are Ruth's aunt and uncle.
- Shadow is Tony and Karrie's cat.
- Ruth is Tony's mother-in-law.
- George is Frieda's brother-in-law.
- Christa is Tony's sister.
- Margaret is Tony's sister-in-law.

1. Who is David? _____

2. Who is Tony? _____

3. How is Kathy related to David and Ruth? _____

4. Who is Ben? _____

5. How is George related to Ben? _____

6. How is Ben related to Henry? _____

7. How is Jack related to Frieda? _____

8. How is Karrie related to Christa? _____

9. How is Tony related to Kathy? _____

10. How is Henry related to Maria? _____

11. Is Karrie related to Margaret? _____

12. How is Tony related to Kevin? _____

13. How are Olaf and Eva related to Kevin? _____

14. How is Henry related to Christa? _____

15. How is George related to Shadow? _____

155. Reasoning from Context

★ Read the paragraph below and then answer the questions with the most reasonable answer.

> Once upon a time there was a strange situation. A baby was found in a cradle on a treetop. This frightened the parents and a group of onlookers from the small community because when the wind blew, the cradle would rock. The crowd worried that if the bough broke, the cradle would fall and down would come baby, cradle and all. As the crowd expanded, the media arrived, along with a local marching band. Someone called 9-1-1. The fire department showed up immediately and saved the child. The band played and the media took pictures. The baby's parents named the child Bo-Peep, and she later went on to have a serious adventure with some lost sheep, but that's another story.

1. What is the topic sentence of the story? _____

_____

2. How do you think the baby arrived at the treetop? _____

_____

3. Why was the crowd frightened or worried? _____

_____

4. Why was it good to have the media at the scene? _____

_____

5. How do you think the fire department saved the child? _____

_____

6. What is 9-1-1? _____

_____

7. Were the parents acting responsibly? Explain your answer. _____

_____

_____

8. What could the community have done to prevent the incident? _____

_____

_____

156. Word Completions: Part One

★ Listed below are 2 sets of 14 words. Use all 26 letters only once per set to complete the words below.

| A B C D E F G H I J K L M N O P Q R S T U V W X Y Z |

Set A

1. S __ U __ ENT
2. __ __ VIGATOR
3. C __ __ CODILE
4. __ E __ AVIOR
5. CHI __ __ EN
6. __ IL __
7. FI __ HT

8. __ ING __ E
9. __ OMB __ E
10. E __ __ LAIN
11. SER __ E
12. __ __ IET
13. __ TO __
14. R __ AD __

| A B C D E F G H I J K L M N O P Q R S T U V W X Y Z |

Set B

1. __ IGZA __
2. __ OM __ LETE
3. TR __ U __ LE
4. __ __ CIDE
5. __ O __ ELY
6. __ IDDE __
7. __ __ CKET

8. __ U __ CKLY
9. __ ON __ EY
10. __ IR __ T
11. __ OW
12. __ __ NNING
13. E __ ACTL __
14. __ HY

157. Word Completions: Part Two

★ Listed below are 2 sets of 14 words. Use all 26 letters only once per set to complete the words below.

A B C D E F G H I J K L M N O P Q R S T U V W X Y Z

SET A

1. __ UESTI __ N
2. __ ORGE __
3. __ ARGON
4. L __ NOLEU __
5. HAP __ __
6. E __ AMI __ E
7. __ E __ O

8. __ UC __ Y
9. __ A __ E
10. __ U __ AR
11. __ __ FINE
12. __ OOKC __ SE
13. __ UG
14. C __ P __ AKE

A B C D E F G H I J K L M N O P Q R S T U V W X Y Z

SET B

1. __ ANY
2. __ NS __ RUMENT
3. INS __ BO __ DINATE
4. F __ RE __ ROUND
5. D __ CREA __ E
6. CI __ ILIZ __ TION
7. __ UREAU __ RACY

8. VO __ ATILE
9. __ OR __ ATION
10. __ ALO __ Y
11. JE __ ELR __
12. __ A __ __ SOME
13. __ UIR __
14. FI __

F--ling -xhaust-d, this l-tt-r has tak-n its-lf out of s-rvic- for on- w--k.

Name_____ Date _____

158. You Should . . . : Part One

★ Each statement below presents a problem with a "You should" at the end. This means you need to think what you "should do" to solve the problem.

★ Write a two-sentence answer for each solution.

1. Your friend Scramblin' Rose has just been named goalie for the high school hockey team. You are cut from that very same team. You should . . .

_____

_____

2. Your dog has fleas, a broken leg, only one eye, no tail, one ear bitten off, and bad breath. His name is "Lucky." You should . . .

_____

_____

3. You are the best looking and smartest student in North America. It bothers you that everyone wants to talk to you. You should . . .

_____

_____

4. Your cow has escaped from the barn. It is twenty minutes past her milking time. You should . . .

_____

_____

5. You have just been told some untrue rumors about your friend. You should . . .

_____

_____

6. Every time you put your hand in your pocket, you pull out ten dollars. You always have money and people are starting to ask questions. You should . . .

_____

_____

159. You Should . . . : Part Two

★ Each statement below presents a problem with a "You should" at the end. This means you need to think what you "should do" to solve the problem.

★ Write a two-sentence answer for each solution.

1. Your friend Scramblin' Rose is offered a singing contract from a music producer. She wants you to be her business manager. You should . . .

_____

_____

_____

2. Scramblin' Rose is offered a 20-million-dollar contract, but she doesn't like to fly to her out-of-town concerts. She asks for your advice. You should . . .

_____

_____

_____

3. Your teacher, whom you usually believe, tells you that he was never a baby. He was 17 at birth. You should . . .

_____

_____

_____

4. You discover that your wimpy-looking brother with the black hair and dark glasses is the superhero who flies around in red-and-blue tights with a big "S" on his chest. You should . . .

_____

_____

_____

5. You discover that your erasable pen works on its own. You just sit there and watch it do all your homework. You are somewhat worried about the amount of ink left in the pen. You should . . .

_____

_____

_____

160. You Should . . . : Part Three

★ Each statement below presents a problem with a "You should" at the end. This means you need to think what you "should do" to solve the problem.

★ Write a two-sentence answer for each solution.

1. Every time you see the number six, you stub your toes, your eyes spin, and your fingers itch. You should . . .

_____

_____

_____

2. Every time you see the number seven, all your pains, spinning, and itchiness disappear. You feel at peace with the world. You should . . .

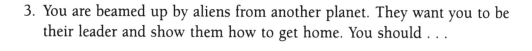

_____

_____

_____

3. You are beamed up by aliens from another planet. They want you to be their leader and show them how to get home. You should . . .

_____

_____

_____

4. This paper you are writing on begins to shimmer and change composition. Slowly it turns into chicken soup. You should . . .

_____

_____

_____

5. Your English composition is so good that your teacher gets it published, and you make a billion dollars. You should . . .

_____

_____

_____

161. The Odd One Out

★ Find the word in each group that does not belong or is the opposite of the others. Write that word in the space provided. Be careful! Words become more difficult as you near the bottom of the page.

1. car, hot rod, automobile, dump truck, airplane _____

2. cow, horse, pig, goat, chicken _____

3. yesterday, never, tomorrow, now, then _____

4. dive, swim, drown, paddle, wade _____

5. records, CDs, tapes, cassettes, elephant _____

6. key, open, close, door, basement _____

7. hubcap, ring, bracelet, jewelry, pendant _____

8. media, bulletin, fear, newspaper, television _____

9. feathers, foam, pillow, sheets, wastebasket _____

10. race, move, flight, sit, run _____

11. work, lazy, power, aggressive, stimulating _____

12. blonde, color, brunette, redhead, auburn _____

13. grumpy, happy, sad, mad, anger _____

14. repulse, love, reject, disavow, disapprove _____

15. dishonesty, integrity, thief, con, bandit _____

16. speckle, speck, blotch, scarf, spot _____

17. ovation, outmoded, applause, tribute, bravo _____

18. overflowing, brimful, empty, overfilled, bursting _____

19. oust, retain, expel, reject, evict _____

20. performance, exercise, dud, rite, ceremony _____

21. motor, transmission, seat, starter, carburetor _____

22. overcome, surmount, hurdle, lose, conquer _____

23. joy, pain, sting, earache, heartburn _____

24. thoughtful, careless, wistful, meditative, melancholic _____

25. phenomenal, remarkable, outstanding, terrible, marvelous _____

HOOKED ON CREATIVE WRITING AND VISUAL EXPRESSION

LEARNING

Name_____ Date _____

162. Creative Writing with Strange Facts: Part One

★ Here are some strange facts. Your job is to circle TRUE or FALSE after each one. You must then support your true or false point of view by explaining "why" you believe the strange fact to be true or false.

1. The genius Albert Einstein was expelled from school.   TRUE   FALSE

   _____

   _____

2. A section of Lombard Street in San Francisco is called the crookedest street in the world. It makes ten sharp turns in only one block.   TRUE   FALSE

   _____

   _____

3. The arms of Napoleon, the Emperor of France, were of different lengths.   TRUE   FALSE

   _____

   _____

4. A skunk can spray its foul-smelling solution accurately at a target twelve feet away.   TRUE   FALSE

   _____

   _____

5. There is a salt mine one thousand feet below the city of Detroit.   TRUE   FALSE

   _____

   _____

6. Ed Schieffelin founded and named the city of Tombstone. He called it this because his friends said he would surely die if he went there.   TRUE   FALSE

   _____

   _____

7. British sailors got their nickname "limey" from their order to drink lemon juice which was called lime juice.   TRUE   FALSE

   _____

   _____

8. Sharks must swim continuously or they will sink.   TRUE   FALSE

   _____

   _____

163. Creative Writing with Strange Facts: Part Two

★ Here are some strange facts. Your job is to circle TRUE or FALSE after each one. You must then support your true or false point of view by explaining "why" you believe the strange fact to be true or false.

1. April Fool's Day started because some people in France refused to switch the start of the year from April 1 to January 1 in 1564. These people were said to be foolish. TRUE FALSE

_____

_____

2. A slug is a snail without a shell.   TRUE   FALSE

_____

_____

3. The word "teenager" did not exist before 1902.   TRUE   FALSE

_____

_____

4. Men are more likely to drown than women.   TRUE   FALSE

_____

_____

5. Cowhide is thicker in North America than in Europe.   TRUE   FALSE

_____

_____

6. The idea for the Frisbee™ was developed from the habit of Yale students tossing pie tins from pies made by the Mother Frisbie's Baking Co. of Bridgeport, Connecticut. TRUE   FALSE

_____

_____

7. A gang of Norwegian thieves carefully used dynamite to crack open a safe. When they got it open, they found it was filled with dynamite!   TRUE   FALSE

_____

_____

8. Egyptian mummies from 1300 B.C. had tattoos.   TRUE   FALSE

_____

_____

Name_____ Date _____

164. Creative Alien Writing

★   Now is your chance to write a letter for these aliens who have arrived from the
    planet Klafluie. They are trying to describe the strange creature they see here.
    They need your help, so use the lines below.

_____

_____

_____

_____

_____

_____

_____

_____

_____

_____

(Continue on the back of this sheet, if necessary.)

165. Recognizing and Making Sentences

★ Some of the sentences below are well-written sentences; others are just groups of words. Find the eight that are *not* sentences and make proper sentences out of them on the lines provided.

1. Joe and dumptruck.

2. The day was nice.

3. Gobomonster and the electronic magazine.

4. Are you playing that "Game Person"?

5. I really do care.

6. Old, green, and fast.

7. Flower power, hippies.

8. Antique, hot rod, backfire.

9. Many fine video games.

10. So many wonderful monsters.

11. Two stories about three.

_____

_____

_____

_____

_____

_____

_____

Name_____ Date _____

166. Avoiding Run-on Sentences: Part One

Quick Access Information ➜ A run-on sentence is one that is tied together with words like *and, so,* and *then*. To correct run-on sentences, you usually need to make shorter meaningful sentences.

★ **Read the paragraph below. It is full of run-on sentences. Rewrite the paragraph in the space provided and change the run-on sentences into shorter meaningful sentences. Continue on the back of this sheet, if necessary.**

Once upon a time a chicken named Henrietta was very upset because she did not know why the sky was blue and she became very anxious to find out so she sought out an intelligent character named Foxy McGillicutty who seemed to "know it all" and so she found him and inquired why the sky was blue. Foxy McGillicutty was intelligent all right and he was also sly and smooth so he convinced Henrietta that the only real way to tell why the sky was blue was to see it from the inside of his huge cooking kettle that was conveniently over a large fire and Henrietta didn't even think twice because Foxy convinced her the heat would give her new insights into this question so she hopped in and it is not known for sure if Henrietta did find out why the sky was blue but one thing is for sure, she doesn't have to be anxious about it anymore and however, Foxy did gain weight.

_____

_____

_____

_____

_____

_____

_____

_____

_____

_____

_____

167. Avoiding Run-on Sentences: Part Two

★ Read the following paragraph. You will see that there are too many "ands." This makes a run-on sentence instead of a proper paragraph.

★ Rewrite the following run-on sentences to make a proper paragraph with shorter sentences. Continue on the back of this sheet, if necessary.

> There was this bright little girl named Mary and she wanted to visit The Big Buster Video Game Station, and she had this one problem however, and it bothered her because she didn't know what to do and the little lamb kept following her into the establishment, and it kept butting the other players and the owners were all upset because the video station was no place for a lamb and even though the lamb was cute and named Butsy Wutsy, Mary had to take her home where she belonged and when Mary returned The Big Buster Video Game Station was closed for the day.

_____

_____

_____

_____

_____

_____

_____

_____

_____

_____

_____

_____

168. Logical Responses: Part One

★ Read each statement. Circle YES if you agree with or support the statement. Circle NO if you disagree with or do not support the statement.

★ Then write why you agree or disagree with the statement. (These points may also be used for class discussions.)

1. There are no environmental problems in the world today. These problems are created by a few scientists looking for attention.   **YES   NO**

_____

_____

_____

2. Drinking and driving is one of the most dangerous habits.   **YES   NO**

_____

_____

_____

3. Who cares about some old rainforest? There are enough trees around here to give us plenty of oxygen.   **YES   NO**

_____

_____

_____

4. We need to pass laws to control pollution.   **YES   NO**

_____

_____

_____

5. Environmental concerns are important for the whole world.   **YES   NO**

_____

_____

_____

Name_____ Date_____

169. Logical Responses: Part Two

★ Read each statement. Circle YES if you agree with or support the statement. Circle NO if you disagree with or do not support the statement.

★ Then write why you agree or disagree with the statements. (These points may also be used for class discussions.)

1. There is no harm drag racing your car in the streets of your town.   YES   NO

_____

_____

_____

2. Drag racing cars should be banned because the spinning and squealing of the tires at the start pollutes the environment.   YES   NO

_____

_____

_____

3. Garbage pollution is a problem found only in the big cities.   YES   NO

_____

_____

_____

4. People are messy by nature, so we shouldn't bother cleaning up.   YES   NO

_____

_____

_____

5. Ozone, "Smozone." Scientists can't get their act together to agree on whether the ozone layer is being depleted or not.   YES   NO

_____

_____

_____

170. One Famous Person Writes to Another: Part One

★ Below is the beginning of a letter from one famous person in history to another. Complete the letter.

September 17, 1787

Dear Jacqueline Kennedy,

    My name is Martha Dandridge Custis Washington. My husband, George, signed a document today that will have an effect on you and your husband John. _____

_____

_____

_____

_____

_____

_____

_____

_____

_____

_____

_____

_____

                     Sincerely,

                     Martha Washington

171. One Famous Person Writes to Another: Part Two

★ Below is the beginning of a letter from one famous person in history to another. Complete the letter.

June 4, 1491

Dear Mr. Abraham Lincoln,

    My name is Christopher Columbus. Next year I am going to discover the New World so you can become _____

_____

_____

_____

_____

_____

_____

_____

_____

_____

_____

_____

_____

Sincerely,

Christopher Columbus

172. Doubling the Creativity

★ Here is an open-ended story from which a colorful picture can be created.

★ Your task is to finish the story on the lines provided and then draw what the story is about in the space below.

   Once upon a time there was a red flower with a green stem growing in a lovely meadow. Suddenly a group of people with heavy-duty yellow construction equipment began to bulldoze the meadow to make room for condominiums. The little red flower cried huge purple tears when he saw the lady driving the earthmover in his direction. The lady felt sorry for the little flower. She got off her machine and began to

_____

_____

_____

173. Constructing Sentences with Keywords

★ Below are groups of three keywords. You are to use each group of keywords to construct or build a well-written sentence.

1. old, young, baby _____

_____

2. pretty, beautiful, ugly _____

_____

3. strong, powerful, weak _____

_____

4. dog, mutt, cat _____

_____

5. early, late, slow _____

_____

6. up, higher, down _____

_____

7. in, inside, out _____

_____

8. edge, brink, middle _____

_____

9. close, shut, open _____

_____

10. blind, dark, see _____

_____

What did you notice about these words? _____

_____

_____

Name_____ Date _____

174. Writing about a Fashion Show

Karrie loves fashion shows, especially when a lot of jewelry is displayed. Today she decides to write a description of last week's Foreign Designer Show at the Pleasant Valley Lodge. Before she starts to write, she thinks about this event and jots down some notes.

★ Here is the start of Karrie's idea list. Use your imagination to add five ideas of your own.

1. <u>The show started with an introduction of the leading foreign designers.</u>

2. _____

3. _____

4. _____

5. _____

6. _____

★ Use these ideas to write the first paragraph in the description of the fashion show at the Pleasant Valley Lodge. Continue on the back, if necessary.

_____

_____

_____

_____

_____

_____

_____

_____

_____

175. Writing about a Video Game

Jason enjoys video games. He decides to write a description of the action in his new video game called *The Rogue Mega Master of Cyberion*. Before Jason starts to write, he thinks about his game and jots down some ideas about the action.

★   Here is the start of Jason's list. Add five ideas of your own.

1.   <u>The game starts with a description of Cyberion and the power of the</u>
     <u>Rogue Mega Master.</u>

2.   _____

3.   _____

4.   _____

5.   _____

6.   _____

★   Use the ideas to write the first paragraph in the description of *The Rogue Mega Master of Cyberion*. Continue on the back, if necessary.

_____

_____

_____

_____

_____

_____

_____

_____

_____

_____

_____

Name_____ Date_____

176. This Is No Accident!

★ **Rewrite each sentence using the word <u>accident</u> somewhere in the sentence.**

1. Bighampton stubbed the big toe on his left foot when the car stopped suddenly.

_____

2. Breanna was driving her car when she stopped suddenly and saw the trouble.

_____

3. The stop sign was finally placed at the corner where the trouble was.

_____

4. When taking driving lessons, you must watch for other cars so you won't smash into them.

_____

5. Bighampton moaned all night after hurting his big toe.

_____

6. Breanna yelled, "Watch out, or you will be sorry!"

_____

7. She had a kerfuffle at the supermarket.

_____

8. Molly had a nice day, free from cares and woes.

_____

9. Breanna thinks girls have less grief when driving than boys do.

_____

10. The woman had driven for years without incident.

_____

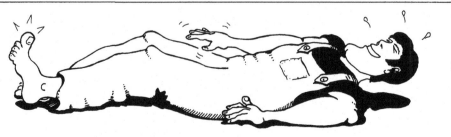

177. Changing the Order of a Sentence

QUICK ACCESS
information

Quick Access Information ➔ Normally the subject (whom or what the sentence is about) comes first. Occasionally a sentence can be made more interesting by putting the predicate (a verb or verb phrase that tells something about the subject) before the subject.

★ **Rewrite the following sentences by putting the predicate before the subject. Here are two examples:**

When the subject begins the sentence ➔	Bighampton wandered into the school.
When the predicate begins the sentence ➔	Into the school wandered Bighampton.

1. The two students drove with wonderful skill.

_____

2. Jamalia walked to the back of the room.

_____

3. Breanna ran into the hall.

_____

4. Akira galloped beside the fence.

_____

5. A muscular man named Tony had come to the dance.

_____

6. Bighampton scurried out the door.

_____

7. The powerful man stood on the stage.

_____

8. Sunshine and Tony talked louder and louder.

_____

Name_____ Date_____

178. Using Correct Language

★ Read the following sentences that are grammatically incorrect. Each contains one or more errors.

★ Rewrite each sentence using correct expressions.

1. Them dogs was all badly behaved.

   _____

2. I couldn't hardly control them.

   _____

3. They sure laid in their cages a time long.

   _____

4. Bighampton, please me to see does puppies.

   _____

5. "I don't gots no dog food no how," Reanna blurted.

   _____

6. Horizon and I think we can learn them some tricks.

   _____

7. I bought a video game off this kid with great graphics.

   _____

8. That dog aren't none different than the mutt I have.

   _____

9. My brother Bartholomew run awayed and began to cry.

   _____

10. I trained my dog to sat down when eatin.

   _____

179. Newspaper Headlines: Part One

★ Here are three newspaper headlines. Each one describes some sort of unusual situation.

★ Your task is to write the rest of the newspaper story in the space provided. Consider the questions *who, what, when, where,* and *why* as you create your newspaper story. (You may use the back of this sheet if you need more space for your stories.)

1. SHORTAGE OF PAPER AND PENS—No More Homework

_____

_____

_____

_____

_____

2. GRAVITY DISAPPEARS, THINGS FLOAT

_____

_____

_____

_____

_____

3. CHICKEN FOUND WITH HUMAN BRAIN—Goes to School

_____

_____

_____

_____

_____

180. Newspaper Headlines: Part Two

★ Here are three newspaper headlines. Each one describes some sort of unusual situation.

★ Your task is to write the rest of the newspaper story in the space provided. Consider the questions *who, what, when, where,* and *why* as you create your newspaper story. (You may use the back of this sheet if you need more space to write.)

1. STUDENT WINS A MILLION DOLLARS—Seeks Advice from Friends on What to Buy

_____

_____

_____

_____

_____

2. NEW PEN DOES SCHOOLWORK FOR STUDENTS—Has Its Own Intelligence

_____

_____

_____

_____

_____

3. STUDENT FIGURES OUT HOW TO MAKE GOLD IN SCIENCE LAB

_____

_____

_____

_____

_____

Name_____ Date _____

181. Applying for a Loan

LOAN APPLICATION FORM

Date _____

Miss
Ms.
Mrs.
Mr. _____
PLEASE PRINT FULL NAME

Date of
Birth _____

Number of
Dependents _____

Home
Address_____
NUMBER AND STREET

Home
Tel. No. _____

Length of Time at Present
Residence _____ yrs.

_____
CITY   STATE   ZIP CODE

Previous Address _____
NUMBER AND STREET   CITY   STATE   ZIP CODE

Nearest relative with
whom not living _____
NAME   ADDRESS   RELATIONSHIP

TOTAL LOAN AMOUNT APPLIED FOR $_____   RATE OF INTEREST _____

PAY BACK TERMS _____/MONTH BEGINNING _____   TERM OF LOAN _____

REASON FOR LOAN _____Checking Account Number is _____

EMPLOYMENT

Present Employer _____

Address _____
STREET   CITY   STATE AND ZIP CODE

Tel. No._____ (Work) _____ (Home)

Social Security Number _____

Annual
Salary $_____ Position _____

Years of Employment _____

Other
Income $_____ Source _____

Previous Employer _____

Years there _____ Reason for Leaving _____

BANK REFERENCES

Checking _____
BANK NAME   BRANCH

_____
BANK NAME   BRANCH

Savings _____
BANK NAME   BRANCH

ADDITIONAL DATA

Spouse's
Name _____   Income $_____

Spouse's
Employer _____
Years of
Employment _____

Real Estate
Location _____   Value $_____

Title in
name of _____   Mortgage $_____

Mortgage
Holder _____
Monthly
Payment $_____

Make and Years of Vehicles _____

Serial #_____

Are there any liens or other legal claims against these vehicles?
☐ Yes ☐ No

Have you applied for
an installment loan
at this Bank previously?

☐ Yes ☐ No

Are there any judgments
or legal proceedings
against you?

☐ Yes ☐ No

List ALL loans or debts on lines below

NAME AND ADDRESS OF CREDITOR	ACCOUNT NUMBER	ORIGINAL AMOUNT	BALANCE UNPAID	MONTHLY PAYMENT

I hereby authorize you to obtain any necessary information from any credit bureau, bank, loan or financial institution that you deem necessary in order to facilitate the approval of this application.

I also hereby state that all information given by me in this application is true and without fault. I understand that any false information will result in the failure of this loan application.

Signature of Applicant _____

Name_____ Date_____

182. Applying for a Driver's License

Name (Last)	(First)	(Middle)	Date

Permanent Address	(Street & Number)	(City)	(State)	Telephone ( )

Present Address	(Street & Number)	(City)	(State)	Telephone ( )

Age	Date of Birth	Social Security Number	State Learner's License Number

Type of License Applied for: Permanent ☐   Temporary ☐   Industrial ☐   Bus ☐   Special ☐

Vitals	Date of Birth ___ ___ ___ mo day yr	Height ___ ft. ___ in.	Hair Color _____	Eye Color _____	Weight _____ lbs.

Considerations - Have you had one of the following conditions:

☐ Heart disease/stroke   ☐ Any condition causing fainting, dizzy spells or unconsciousness

☐ Convulsions   ☐ Mental illness

☐ Epilepsy   ☐ Physical disability in any part of the body

Do you wear corrective lenses? ☐ Yes ☐ No	Contact lenses? ☐ Yes ☐ No

Do you have a valid driver's license from this or any other state, Canadian province or other country?

☐ Yes   ☐ No

If yes, state/province and country and number on license _____

Have you ever had a driver's license or permit refused, suspended or taken away?

☐ Yes   ☐ No

Do you require a verbal examination?

☐ Yes   ☐ No

Signature of Applicant _____

Age Verification

Please attach original copy (to be returned) of one of the following:

Birth Certificate ☐   Passport ☐   Baptismal Certificate ☐   Affidavit ☐

183. Applying for Employment

NAME IN FULL	MR. MRS. MISS MS.	LAST	FIRST	MIDDLE	MAIDEN NAME	SOC. SEC. NO.
NUMBER AND STREET			CITY	STATE	ZIP	TELEPHONE NO.

MARITAL STATUS		DATE OF BIRTH	MO.	DAY	YR.

POSITION APPLIED FOR		DATE

HEIGHT	WEIGHT	WEAR GLASSES ☐ YES ☐ NO	ANY PHYSICAL DEFECTS ☐ YES ☐ NO	EXPLAIN

EDUCATIONAL EXPERIENCE

TYPE OF SCHOOL	NAME AND ADDRESS	YRS. ATTENDED	WHEN LEFT	MAJOR AREAS OF STUDY
ELEMENTARY OR GRADE				
HIGH SCHOOL				
COLLEGE				
BUSINESS OR TRADE				

WORK SKILLS

WHAT KIND OF WORK DO YOU LIKE?	TYPING SPEED
DESCRIBE MACHINES/COMPUTER PROGRAMS YOU KNOW HOW TO USE.	SHORTHAND SPEED

IN CASE OF EMERGENCY NOTIFY	NAME	RELATIONSHIP
	ADDRESS	TELEPHONE NO.

PREVIOUS WORK RECORD

INDICATE LAST OR PRESENT EMPLOYER FIRST

DATES FROM TO	EMPLOYER	PAY SCALE START FINISH	JOB TITLE AND SUPERVISOR'S NAME	REASON FOR LEAVING
	NAME			
	ADDRESS			
	NAME			
	ADDRESS			
	NAME			
	ADDRESS			

REFERENCES (Non-Relative)

	NAME	ADDRESS	OCCUPATION
1.			
2.			

False statements are grounds for dismissal.

DATE _____ SIGNATURE _____

184. Writing a Friendly Letter

HEADING ————————————⌐1811 West 34th Street
                      │Cody, WY 70758
                      └January 2, 2003

GREETING ———————⌐Dear Beanie,

BODY ——————⌐   We are going to the Daytona 500 Stock Car Race this
           │year in Daytona Beach, Florida. The race is on Sunday,
           │January 20, 2003.
           │   If you decide to join us, we will book a hotel room for
           │you. It will be a great time with our friends.
           └   Please try to make it if you can.

CLOSING ———————————⌐Your pal,

SIGNATURE ———————————⌐John Henry

1. Name the five major parts of the friendly letter: _____

_____

2. What type of punctuation comes after the name of the town or city?

_____

3. What type of punctuation comes after the greeting? _____

4. What type of punctuation comes after the closing? _____

5. The closing is directly in line with the _____.

6. The indented words in the body line up under what word? _____

7. The second line of the body is in line with what word? _____

8. What word in the closing does not have a capital letter? _____

185. Designing a Bicycle Seat

★ It has often been said that the bicycle seat is the world's worst product. It is hard, you can barely sit on it, and it usually hurts.

★ Your task is to design (draw) and describe a totally new bike seat for the world to use.

★ Your new bike seat design must meet the following criteria:

1. It must be practical or useful.
2. It must be cost effective or low cost to produce.
3. It must be comfortable.

DRAWING:

WRITTEN DESCRIPTION:

_____

_____

_____

_____

_____

_____

_____

_____

Use the back of this sheet if you need more space for your description.

186. Designing a Hot Rod

★ It's time to let your creative skills go to work. Design your own hot rod or street rod.

★ To build your car, redesign any of its current features (grill, headlights, hubcaps, or other) and put any or all of the following items on your machine: flames, stripes, stars, flowers, louvers, aerials with foxtails, weird color schemes, or anything else you feel would make your car the finest example of "cool."

★ An editor from *Car Magazine* will call you for a description of the special features of your newly designed machine. At the bottom of the page, list the features (nouns) and describe each one, using one to three adjectives for each.

SPECIAL FEATURE	DESCRIPTION

187. I Say the Earth Is Flat

★ Many people thought Earth was flat before Christopher Columbus discovered the New World. There is a Flat Earth Society in London, England that still tries to say the Earth is flat. Consider yourself to be a member of that society.

★ Draw your idea of how the world would look if it were flat. Describe special features of your flat Earth in the space below.

SPECIAL FEATURE	DESCRIPTION

188. Creating an Ad

★ The following is an advertisement to sell frozen apple pies.

★ Notice the layout, content, and heading. The content has only two complete sentences. The first four bullets are phrases that make a complete sentence when added to "We offer." Follow this layout for your ad.

★ Your job is to design an ad (in the box below) to sell one of your (or your friend's) old smelly sneakers.

ESTHER'S FROZEN APPLE PIES

Now is the Time to Buy, Buy, Buy!

We offer:

- Only the best sliced apples
- Tender and flaky, top-quality crusts
- Pies baked to perfection
- Sweet homemade flavor
- Buy Esther's Pies at stores everywhere or phone 201-555-2121 for free delivery

189. Opening and Closing a Paragraph

> Quick Access Information ➔ The opening sentence of a paragraph is often the topic sentence that states the main idea. The closing or last sentence ties the paragraph together in a complete package.

★ Here are the opening, or topic sentence, and the closing, or last sentence, of a paragraph. Your task is to fill in the middle of the paragraph.

Bighampton Butler Jones frightened everyone in town when he took flying lessons.

_____

_____

_____

_____

_____

Everyone breathed a sigh of relief when the airplane landed safely.

★ In the paragraph below, you must add the first, or topic sentence, and the last, or closing sentence, of the paragraph.

_____

_____

_____

Akira did not know what to do with the oobladoink. He began to sweat when it started to spin and whistle. He even asked Molly and Sonia if it was safe to approach the expanding mechanical creature. _____

_____

_____

190. Writing Paragraphs

Quick Access Information ➜ A good paragraph deals with only one topic. You must have a new paragraph for every change of speaker.

★ **Rewrite the following story on another sheet of paper, separating it into proper paragraphs.**

ONCE UPON A TIME

Once upon a time, long ago and far away (actually it was last year in Pough-keepsie), a cow, a cat, a plate, and a spoon all had the same goal. They wanted more happiness and excitement in their lives. "I think I'll jump over the moon," Bossy the Cow said with assurance as she looked at the sky. Diddle Diddle the Cat stated, "That's a wonderful idea, but to have long-lasting excitement, I will learn to play the fiddle." The Plate and the Spoon both said they wanted more contentment in their lives and to not be thought of as just utensils! "It can't be done," Buster the Dog criticized. "You are all foolish," he blurted as he laughed at them. After several attempts Bossy finally succeeded and earned everlasting fame in a nursery rhyme. Buster often made fun of Diddle Diddle as he practiced many hours on the fiddle. This made Diddle Diddle's work long and hard but eventually he too succeeded and became an international star. Buster really barked nasty things at Heather the Plate and Darryl B. Spoon, but they left Buster behind as they ran away together. Heather found Darryl B. to be sweet because he was always full of sugar and Darryl thought Heather was a real dish, so they lived happily ever after in a setting of their own. Moral of the Story: Don't let the Busters of this world step on your dreams. They are usually barking up the wrong tree.

ANSWER KEY

SECTION 1

1. Developing Vocabulary: Part One

1. big
2. huge
3. worry
4. manage
5. a person, place, or thing
6. virtue
7. concentrate
8. liquid
9. remove
10. desire
11. dress
12. weight
13. fumble
14. ghastly
15. persistent
16. corrosive
17. glorify
18. storm
19. bend
20. glowing

2. Developing Vocabulary: Part Two

Answers will vary.

3. Solving Word Problems: Part One

Middle words will vary. Synonyms for *Happiness*: contentment, delight, pleasure, gladness, blissfulness, cheerfulness.

4. Solving Word Problems: Part Two

Middle words will vary. Synonyms for *Awesome*: fantastic, wonderful, superb, marvelous, outstanding, fabulous.

5. Letter Replacements

1. beat
2. neat
3. assistance
4. rate
5. demonstrate
6. distance
7. safety
8. salute
9. teacher
10. tavern
11. tasteless
12. importance
13. teenager
14. tide
15. tinsel
16. bisect
17. tie-dye
18. adjective
19. tiger
20. mention
21. electric
22. indecent
23. generosity
24. invite

6. Video-Game Consonant Search

1. electronic
2. star
3. online
4. invader
5. thrill
6. alien
7. adventure
8. power
9. launch
10. rogue
11. opponent
12. mega
13. worm
14. dragon
15. heat
16. extreme
17. shiver
18. gaming
19. action
20. metal

7. Word Builder with Letter "W"

Possible answers:

1. wrath	8. within	15. wedlock	21. washup
2. well behaved	9. whisker	16. warped	22. whatever
3. wrench	10. windjammer	17. webquest	23. workweek
4. wildcat	11. walking	18. wardroom	24. waxen
5. whether	12. walnut	19. waist	25. wayward
6. wife	13. warmup	20. wiretap	26. wizard
7. weight	14. witness		

8. Ice Hockey Vocabulary

1. puck	7. Stanley Cup	14. knee & shin pads	20. goalie pads
2. goalie	8. Bruins	15. penalty box	21. chest pads
3. red	9. gloves	16. arena	22. shoulder pads
4. fans	10. helmet	17. practice	23. boards
5. period	11. tape	18. B	24. two minutes
6. coach	12. cage	19. six	25. stick
	13. skates		

9. Pick a Sport: Part One

1. baseball	5. football	8. skydiving
2. volleyball	6. weightlifting	9. archery
3. javelin	7. table tennis	10. mountain climbing
4. golf		

10. Pick a Sport: Part Two

1. skiing	5. shot put	8. badminton
2. bowling	6. basketball	9. fencing
3. hockey	7. swimming	10. tennis
4. discus		

11. Grouping Sports Vocabulary

Answers will vary. Some possible answers are:

1. slam dunk, Celtics, center, field goal, net, floor, shoot
2. puck, skate, blade, net, center, shoot, helmet, left wing
3. racket, love, net, out, set, grip, serve
4. out, strike, slider, helmet, pitch, homer
5. field goal, 50-yard line, touchdown, center, helmet, pigskin

6. Tour de France, pedals, helmet, wheel

7. mogul, poles, wax

8. spike, serve, set, out, net, floor

9. green, tee, putter, grip

10. parachute, ripcord, gravity, helmet

11. engine, wheel, power, helmet

12. muscles, wrist, upper body strength

13. hull, propeller, anchor, engine, bail, power

14. gutter, pins, alley, strike

15. bow, arrow, target, shoot

12. Sports Spelling

1. touchdown
2. homerun
3. hole-in-one
4. racquet
5. slam dunk
6. crosscheck
7. marathon
8. freestyle
9. board
10. Indianapolis 500
11. field goal
12. thoroughbred
13. butterfly
14. travel
15. lure
16. bench press
17. parachute
18. hang ten
19. mogul
20. dribble
21. tuna
22. skates
23. third base
24. tee off
25. engine

13. The Great Search for "Out" Words

1. outpatient
2. outdated
3. outside
4. outlook
5. output
6. outrage
7. outride
8. outreach
9. outrun
10. outshine
11. outtalk
12. outvote
13. outshoot
14. outset
15. outrank
16. outsize
17. outscore
18. outmost
19. outspoken
20. outfox/outsmart

14. Boxed Vocabulary Creation

1. cream
2. or
3. car
4. gem (or get)
5. cage
6. game
7. are
8. spite (or score)
9. picky
10. score (or spite)
11. get (or gem)
12. more (or make)
13. make (or more)
14. bite (or back or bare)
15. back (or bite or bare)
16. bare (or bite or back)
17. bay
18. sick (or sock or seam)
19. sock (or sick or seam)
20. seam (or sick or sock)

15. Workers' Vocabulary Puzzle: Part One

1. F A R M E R S
2. S P O I L
3. T I R E D
4. D E P O S I T
5. E L E P H A N T S
6. L E A V E
7. A I R P L A N E S
8. R E P A I R E D
9. I N F O R M A T I O N
10. S H A R I N G
11. F R U I T
12. H A N D S

16. Workers' Vocabulary Puzzle: Part Two

1. P A Y
2. L A Z Y
3. E Y E
4. E N V E L O P E S
5. O L D E R
6. P E O P L E
7. M O N E Y
8. A R R I V I N G
9. L E F T
10. T Y I N G
11. R I C H
12. E A T

17. Work-World Vocabulary: Part One

1. communicate
2. stove
3. teeth
4. computers
5. shoes
6. change
7. listen

18. Work-World Vocabulary: Part Two

1. fight
2. steal
3. police officers
4. manager
5. state fairs
6. robots
7. face shields

19. Employment Vocabulary

Answers will vary.

20. Choosing Work-Related Vocabulary: Part One

1. surgeons
2. informal
3. costumes
4. ear plugs
5. flippers
6. buttons
7. detectives
8. gloves
9. laces
10. jockeys

21. Choosing Work-Related Vocabulary: Part Two

1. hard hats
2. work boots
3. earrings
4. rubber gloves
5. parkas
6. oil
7. police
8. face shields
9. watch
10. tire

22. Positive Vocabulary Puzzle

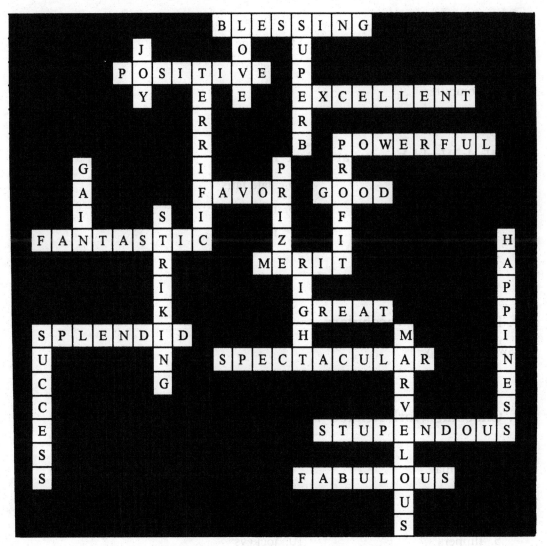

23. Word Builder—Deceptive Words

Answers will vary.

24. Word Builder—Exciting Words

Answers will vary.

25. Rich Word Puzzle

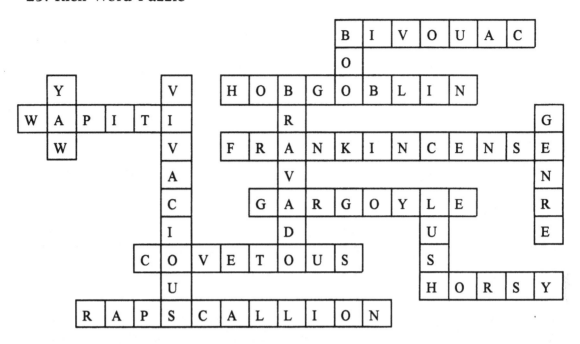

26. The Wright Brothers and Spelling

1. flight
2. airplane
3. Orville
4. kite
5. glider
6. bicycle
7. air
8. Kitty Hawk
9. Van Cleve
10. wind
11. Wilbur
12. flying
13. wing
14. repairs
15. pilot
16. tunnel
17. brothers
18. machine
19. interest
20. successful

Extra Credit: The reflection of the Wright Brothers' plane is on the face shield of the astronaut.

27. Auto Vocabulary

1. Driving
2. Races
3. Alcohol
4. Gas
5. Speedways
6. Tires
7. Elapsed
8. Reverse
9. Horses
10. Old
11. Transmission
12. Rear
13. Oval
14. Drivers

28. Hot-Rod Vocabulary Every Teenager Should Know

1. King Kong
2. headers
3. mags
4. 23T Bucket
5. torque
6. Corvette
7. scoop
8. V8
9. pit crew
10. Deuce Coupe
11. Mustang
12. Salt Flats, Utah
13. street rods
14. burned rubber
15. horsepower

29. Auto Vocabulary for a Mobile Society

1. hood
2. mag wheels
3. door panel
4. carburetor
5. trunk
6. seat belts
7. ignition switch
8. horn button
9. hood ornament
10. headlights
11. distributor
12. head liner
13. spindle
14. air bag
15. windshield
16. wiring harness
17. muffler
18. gauges
19. transmission
20. air cleaner
21. radiator
22. motor
23. hubcaps
24. grill
25. body

30. Plymouth Colony Reinforcers

1.

A	P	C	O	M
T	D	E	W	P
T	Q	B	I	A
A	U	T	L	C
L	O	L	V	J

A	M	R	W	V
X	P	U	E	I
U	F	R	O	T
V	T	E	B	K
S	A	N	Y	M

P	J	N	O	P
L	L	U	C	E
G	H	G	T	T
B	C	J	R	N
D	Y	N	L	M

2. HOLLAND
   EFFECT
   SETTLE

   PERMISSION
   OPPRESSIVE
   FREEDOM

   SLEEPING
   SPEEDWELL
   FINALLY

3. SHIP
   VOYAGE
   MAYFLOWER

   FAITH
   FREEDOM
   COURAGE

SECTION 2

31. Important Definitions Made Easy
No answers required.

32. Identifying English Grammar

elephant	evade	eventually	elegant
Norman	navigate	newly	new
goulash	grow	greatly	green
lettuce	lift	lately	little
India	introduce	internally	inner
sugar	shut	slowly	solid
hat	hum	happily	hard

33. Common and Proper Nouns: Part One

1. T	6. O	11. A	16. C
2. O	7. O	12. Y	17. H
3. B	8. L	13. I	18. O
4. E	9. S	14. N	19. O
5. C	10. T	15. S	20. L

Important truth: To be cool, stay in school.

34. Common and Proper Nouns: Part Two

hot dog	Asia	Doctor Smith
Red Rock River	river	peacock
Gattleburg	Lady Diana	sparrow
Virginia	Queen Elizabeth	rooster
Benedict Arnold	cowbell	Great Salt Lake
Missouri River	Marybell	July
airplane	Pittsburgh	Wednesday
lucky lady	Park Avenue	Kathy
rubber boot	dogs	Boise
Jason's rubber boot	Washington Irving	taxes
George Washington	trains	queen
Bay of Bengal	lake	servant
Dallas Cowboys	woman	Clara Cow
Mississippi River		

35. Buckets of Words
Students should write five each of the following words.

NOUNS	VERBS	ADJECTIVES	ADVERBS
car	squealed	green	menacingly
tires	chased	funny	forcefully
cow	may	old	hopefully
teenager	asked	blue	slowly
teacher	ate	giant	lovingly
snooze	cared	tiny	quickly
class	stampeded	wild	proudly
Bighampton	is	best	confidently
bug	are	teenage	usually
fly	said	intelligent	bashfully
Kathy	wear	people	arrogantly
baby	bragged	purple	
horses	was	polka-dot	
schoolyard		party	
United States		awesome	
country		cool	
world			
boys			
Bobby			
eaters			
bikinis			
Jamalia			
Molly			
dress			

36. Identifying Nouns, Verbs, and Adjectives

1. noun
2. adjective
3. adjective
4. verb
5. adjective
6. noun
7. adjective
8. verb
9. noun
10. adjective
11. adjective
12. noun

37. Adjective Power
Rewritten sentence answers will vary. Adjectives to be circled are:

2. that, golden
3. more, wonderful, large
4. delicious, goose
5. cute
6. Goose, good, sweet, pure
7. valuable, golden
8. real, just, Fool's
9. big, real, shiny, heavy
10. strange, golden, weighty, huge
11. nutritious, less, valuable
12. brilliant, marvelous

38. The Wonderful World of Adjectives and Adverbs

Answers will vary.

39. Using Adjectives on the *Titanic*

Answers will vary.

40. Adverbs for Akira and Sonia

ADVERB	NEW ADVERB
1. quickly	Answers will vary.
2. happily	
3. safely	
4. furiously	
5. surprisingly	
6. correctly	
7. wisely	
8. temporarily	
9. emotionally	
10. fearfully	

41. Pronouns with Molly Sousa and Flipper Twerpski

She	Everyone	she	she
her	they	them	You
She	their	her	She
He	her	it	He
her	She	she	her

42. Plurals of Nouns

No answers required.

43. Plural Puzzle: Part One

1. children	6. women
2. heroes	7. ladies
3. calves	8. mice
4. pigs	9. boys
5. oxen	10. dollies

44. Plural Puzzle: Part Two

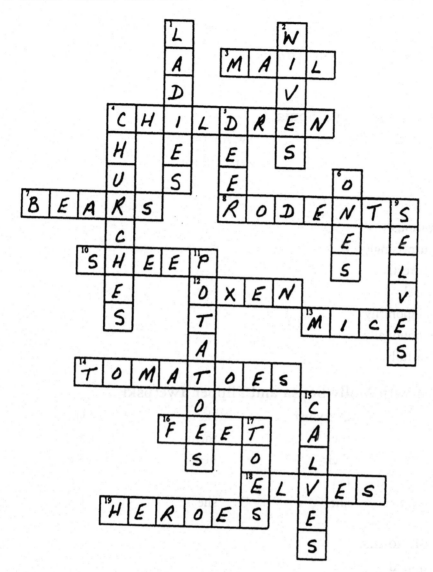

45. Making Nouns Plural: Part One

1. trucks
2. joysticks
3. monitors
4. birches
5. loaves
6. pianos
7. pluses
8. babies
9. classes
10. writers in residence
11. jockeys
12. scarves
13. radios
14. potatoes
15. oxen
16. pants
17. oddities
18. children
19. witches
20. camels

46. Making Nouns Plural: Part Two

1. daughters-in-law
2. lives
3. loaves
4. sleighs
5. monsters
6. Internet
7. mosses
8. turkeys
9. sheep
10. leaves
11. cities
12. teeth
13. calves
14. lamps
15. horses
16. lemons
17. monkeys
18. ladies-in-waiting
19. queens
20. fears

47. Collective Nouns

1. class
2. council
3. school
4. bouquet
5. Fleet
6. regiment
7. squadron
8. team
9. gang
10. club
11. group
12. union
13. plethora
14. organization
15. committee

48. Contractions—The Long and the Short of It

1. haven't
2. he's
3. you're
4. they're
5. who's
6. won't
7. don't
8. he'd
9. can't
10. she'll
11. it's
12. I'm
13. aren't
14. let's
15. we've

49. Contraction Use in Sentences

1. Haven't
2. We've
3. Let's
4. She'll
5. Won't
6. Aren't
7. It's
8. Don't
9. Can't
10. Who's
11. They're
12. You're (or He's)
13. He's (or You're or I'm)
14. He's
15. I'm (You're or They're or He's)

50. The Great Abbreviation Page

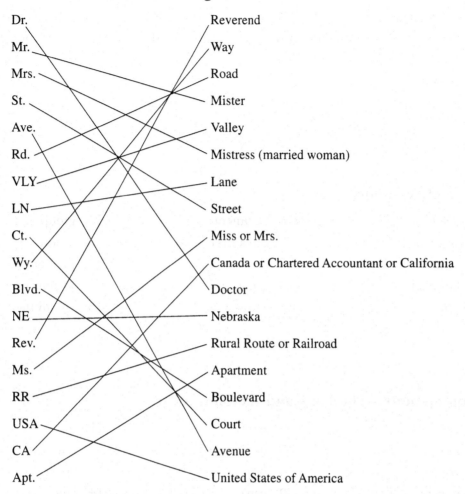

Dr.	Reverend
Mr.	Way
Mrs.	Road
St.	Mister
Ave.	Valley
Rd.	Mistress (married woman)
VLY	Lane
LN	Street
Ct.	Miss or Mrs.
Wy.	Canada or Chartered Accountant or California
Blvd.	Doctor
NE	Nebraska
Rev.	Rural Route or Railroad
Ms.	Apartment
RR	Boulevard
USA	Court
CA	Avenue
Apt.	United States of America

51. Choosing Synonyms—Words that Mean the Same

1. rubbish	6. hideous	11. force	16. beauty
2. automobile	7. hilarious	12. fighting	17. animal
3. investigate	8. heaven	13. dishonesty	18. anger
4. intoxicated	9. forbidden	14. black	19. amusement
5. invention	10. foreigner	15. bend	20. actor

52. The Difference Among Synonyms, Homonyms, and Antonyms

1. S	10. S	19. A	28. H	37. H
2. H	11. S (or A)	20. S	29. S	38. A
3. A	12. A	21. S	30. S	39. A
4. A	13. A	22. H	31. S	40. A
5. A	14. A	23. S	32. A	41. A
6. A	15. S	24. S	33. H	42. A
7. H	16. A	25. A	34. A	43. S
8. H	17. H	26. S	35. S	44. S
9. A	18. H	27. S	36. S	

53. The Wonderful Antonym Puzzle

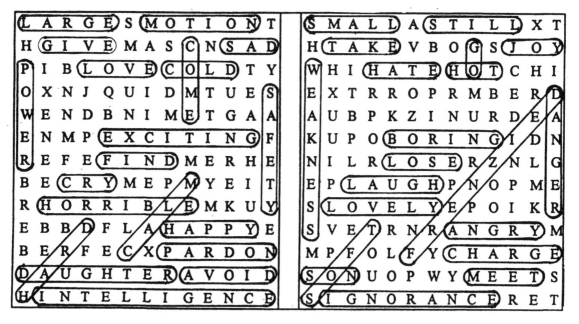

1. small
2. motion
3. exciting
4. pardon
5. frenzied

6. meet
7. angry
8. safety
9. ignorance
10. hard

11. go
12. horrible
13. cry
14. take
15. weakness

16. hate
17. daughter
18. lose
19. hot
20. sad

54. Overworked, Tired, and Worn-out Synonyms

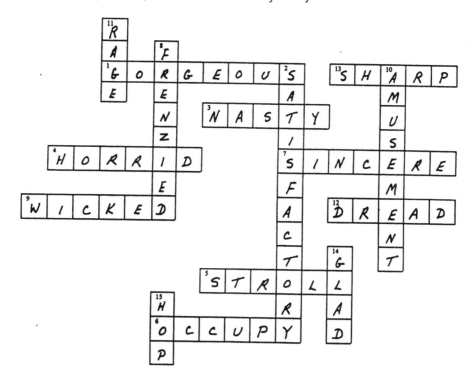

55. Picking "P"-Word Synonyms Perfectly

1. (b) purse
2. (a) dive
3. (b) feathers
4. (c) implore
5. (b) village green
6. (c) ravage
7. (b) corpulent

8. (a) stance
9. (b) impoverishment
10. (a) hypothesis
11. (c) useful
12. (b) preference
13. (c) introduction

14. (a) valuable
15. (c) grounds
16. (a) put on trial
17. (a) supporter
18. (c) fraud
19. (b) disturb
20. (b) peaceful

21. (c) soap box
22. (a) rich wealthy class
23. (b) vertical
24. (c) scheme
25. (a) pick or gather

56. The Homonym Puzzle

B	S	E	M	N	P	O	L	W	Q	U	H	P	O	M	B	L	N	I
N	J	G	N	H	I	L	U	W	A	L	O	U	D	N	L	H	F	G
B	I	L	P	O	R	W	E	S	T	D	U	M	V	W	I	U	L	K
K	L	O	M	P	C	N	M	D	E	E	R	W	C	D	R	E	W	M
T	R	W	I	V	S	B	M	R	I	O	S	R	V	U	E	N	A	C
R	G	H	M	T	E	M	B	U	G	E	Y	V	B	M	W	A	I	T
N	L	K	S	J	E	B	T	E	H	B	W	H	O	L	E	V	S	R
Y	W	K	J	K	N	I	G	H	T	P	O	E	I	M	E	N	T	O
P	L	A	I	N	Y	W	X	E	R	T	E	A	W	C	K	P	V	W
I	C	W	L	O	R	B	B	A	R	E	V	L	D	E	V	R	I	P
X	K	N	E	W	E	S	B	R	U	A	K	L	E	V	C	I	D	R
C	R	W	A	J	L	E	A	D	O	M	R	W	C	A	N	T	I	B
K	E	L	P	E	W	A	M	T	L	N	O	L	S	C	W	E	T	L

aloud	heard	or	tea
eight	whole	hours	team
ant	lead	plain	to
bare	knew	write	waist
deer	knight	seen	week
heal	know	sea	wait

57. Two-Function Synonym Puzzle

alarm, dread, fear, panic, worry

brisk, fast, quick, rapid, swift

error, fault, flaw, lapse, slip

58. Synonym and Antonym Grids

1.

SYNONYMS	ANTONYMS
firm	soft
tough	tender
rigid	limp

2.

B	E	N	A	S	T	Y	W	O	P	K	E
G	A	W	F	U	L	G	N	E	M	L	R
R	O	T	T	E	N	J	O	R	V	U	M
E	M	A	V	T	I	K	T	O	T	I	P
A	K	O	C	Y	C	P	Y	S	D	S	L
T	L	P	W	M	E	L	N	O	E	W	U

SYNONYMS

evil
awful
nasty
rotten

ANTONYMS

nice
good
lovely
great

3.

L	O	C	K	U	P	R	T	A	G	U	H
E	G	A	C	J	A	I	L	R	T	N	S
O	P	K	E	R	M	V	N	R	V	T	D
L	I	B	E	R	T	Y	S	E	W	I	C
U	W	V	E	B	D	G	F	S	D	E	M
S	Y	P	R	I	S	O	N	T	W	T	N

SYNONYMS

liberty
untie
permit

ANTONYMS

lockup
jail
prison
arrest
cage

59. Compound Words

1. afternoon	afterhours	afterlife	aftermath
2. waterwheel	underwater	water-logged	watermelon
3. bluebell	bluegrass	bluebonnet	blueprint
4. hairbrush	hairdo	hairline	haircut
5. everyone	oneself	anyone	onetime
6. dogwood	dogcatcher	doghouse	dog-tired
7. seaport	seaplane	seamen	seafood
8. airfield	airspace	aircraft	airplane
9. lovesick	love-nest	truelove	lovebird
10. blackbird	songbird	birdbrain	birdbath
11. houseboat	housecleaner	household	housefly
12. firecracker	firestorm	firearm	backfire
13. freewill	freestyle	freewheel	freeway
14. catfish	catnip	tomcat	cattail
15. deathbed	deathwatch	deathblow	deathtrap

60. Developing Compound Words

1. steamboat	8. mailbox	14. spyglass	20. bedspread
2. horseshoe	9. thoroughbred	15. oversight	21. commonplace
3. keepsake	10. zigzag	16. loophole	22. merrymaking
4. baseball	11. dollhouse	17. snowbound	23. safeguard
5. lifeguard	12. teamwork	18. wheelbarrow	24. salesperson
6. wrongdoing	13. storyteller	19. sleepwalking	25. grasshopper
7. sweetheart			

61. Compound Sets

1. over	6. love	11. hot
2. out	7. long	12. house
3. sun	8. fire	13. green
4. back	9. light	14. hard
5. hand	10. free	15. head

62. Constructing Compound Words

1. over	5. hand	9. hot
2. out	6. love	10. house
3. star	7. long	11. green
4. mail	8. head	12. hard

63. Making the Most of Similes

Answers will vary.

64. Making the Most of Metaphors

Answers will vary.

65. Writing Conversation: Part One

No answers required.

66. Writing Conversation: Part Two

No answers required.

67. Writing Conversation: Part Three

No answers required.

68. Writing What Someone Says: Part One

2. "Give her the hairbrush and the mirror," <u>her boyfriend, Bighampton, timidly suggested</u>.

3. "I just wanted to see how pretty I am," <u>said Breanna</u>.

4. "You may be pretty, but I'm smart," <u>Sonia blurted in defense</u>.

5. "We've got to do something about Breanna," <u>Mike said to Bighampton</u>.

6. "Yes, she's got a big head," <u>Molly interjected</u>.

7. "Arrogant people turn me off," <u>said Mike</u>.

8. "When you're this pretty, it's easy to admire yourself," <u>Breanna interrupted</u>.

9. "I can't say much because I'm her boyfriend," <u>Bighampton said cowardly</u>.

10. "People should just admit and accept the fact that I'm a beautiful person," <u>Breanna said proudly</u>.

11. "This is hard to take," <u>Mike observed</u>.

12. "That's for sure," <u>everyone responded at the same time</u>.

69. Writing What Someone Says: Part Two

2. <u>Akira replied</u>, "You will never get another chance."

3. <u>Karrie looked at the plane and stated</u>, "You're frightened because this plane is over sixty years old."

4. <u>Bighampton blurted</u>, "I'm scared and I have a right to be."

5. <u>Akira looked at his friends and said</u>, "But it's been fully restored."

6. <u>Bighampton, shaking with fear, said</u>, "It's not the actual safe flying that bothers me."

7. <u>Bighampton continued</u>, "I'm more concerned about how the plane comes down."

8. <u>Karrie looked at the large wings and said</u>, "It is heavier than air."

9. <u>Breanna looked at Bighampton and cooed</u>, "Will you do it for me?"

10. <u>Akira looked at Bighampton and mocked</u>, "Come on, scaredy cat."

11. <u>Karrie retorted</u>, "I kind of agree with Bighampton."

12. <u>Breathing a sigh of relief, Bighampton blurted</u>, "I never argue with a lady who has the correct point of view."

70. Writing What Someone Says: Part Three

1. "Are you waiting for Bighampton?" asked Akira.

2. "Wow, Breanna, you sure are strong," blurted Akira.

3. Breanna retorted, "Are you teasing me?"

4. Akira shouted suddenly, "Don't move!"

5. Akira asked, "May I take your picture?"

6. "Stop teasing me," Breanna shrieked.

7. "Is Bighampton back from his muscle-building workout?" Breanna queried.

8. "Just wait till I get my hands on him," Breanna grumbled.

9. "Does he cater to your every whim and request?" Akira asked.

10. "He hasn't catered to every whim or request," Breanna replied. "Once in grade five several years ago, he didn't pick up a pencil for me."

71. Writing What Someone Says: Part Four

"Hi, Big Bad," Mr. Bear stated. "How are you feeling today?"

"Oh, greetings, Mr. Bear," Big Bad Wolf replied, "my bones ache but other than that I'm okay."

Suddenly Mr. Bear blurted, "Say, do you remember the grief I had because of that little girl with the strange name?"

"What do you mean, strange name?" Wolf cackled through his loose false teeth.

"Well," Mr. Bear surmised, "how does Goldilocks sound to you?"

Big Bad Wolf pondered for a moment and said, "That's a strange name, all right. Come to think of it, I had trouble with a little girl with a strange name too."

"What was it?" Mr. Bear asked.

"Little Red Riding Hood," Big Bad responded. "I also had some misfortune with three little pigs," Wolf went on, "but that's another story."

Mr. Bear perked up and said, "I heard those three pigs are in the Cozy Sty Nursing Home on Pasadena Blvd. What do you say we go over there and cause some trouble for old time's sake?"

Big Bad looked Mr. Bear in the face and said, "What with my rheumatism, arthritis, and lack of teeth, I'd sooner stay for dinner here in the home."

"Come to think of it," Mr. Bear replied, "let's stay here and relax."

SECTION 3

72. Understanding Root, Prefix, and Suffix

WORD	ROOT	PREFIX	SUFFIX
unlovely	love	un	ly
lurching	lurch	—	ing
crusty	crust	—	y
ascertained	ascertain	—	ed
perky	perk	—	y
lucky	luck	—	y
utterly	utter	—	ly
uncluttered	clutter	un	ed
belabored	labor	be	ed
unpublished	publish	un	ed
shadowiness	shadow	—	iness
unhandy	hand	un	y
disapprove	approve	dis	—
adventuring	adventure	—	ing
exchanged	change	ex	ed
disliked	like	dis	ed
returning	turn	re	ing
anticlimax	climax	anti	—
backer	back	—	er
friskier	frisk	—	ier

73. Selfish Hyphenated Words

1. self-respect
2. self-righteous
3. self-denial
4. self-interest
5. self-seeking
6. self-sacrifice
7. self-conscious
8. self-esteem
9. self-taught
10. self-starter
11. self-winding
12. self-improvement
13. self-indulgent
14. self-supporting
15. self-willed

74. Pretty "Pre" Words

1. precise
2. preconception
3. prejudice
4. prepare
5. predetermined
6. predict
7. predicament
8. predominance
9. predominate
10. precipitation
11. precious
12. precinct
13. precipice
14. precarious
15. preacher

75. Learning about Syllables

Possible answers:

ONE-SYLLABLE WORDS		TWO-SYLLABLE WORDS		THREE-SYLLABLE WORDS	
once	pond	up·on	walk·ing	to·tal·ly	how·ev·er
class	cool	him·self	brain·wave	teen·ag·er	Big·hamp·ton
time	field	be·cause	per·son	sud·den·ly	be·hav·ior
there	school	back·wards	sur·mised	eve·ry·thing	re·al·ize
strange	wore	plen·ty	a·round	in·stant·ly	i·de·a

76. Proofreading for Capitals

1.   J   S   C   W
jamalia sousa was at the museum in cody, wyoming.

2.   E   A   B   I
eugene aulinger is the best conductor of bernstein i have ever seen.

3.   R B   R
rick benson's composition of the musical piece called riel is a masterpiece.

4.   T   P   B   D   B
"the video game, *power blasted doorbells*, just rings my chimes," said bighampton.

5.   T M   R   B   M
the missouri river flows near billings, montana.

6.   T   USS U   S   N   Y
the ship uss united states must begin stopping twenty-five miles from new york.

7.   K   I   C   O   G
karrie and i went to the chinese olympic games.

8.   T A   H   N   N   F   D
the anthony hotel was saved by the newport news fire department.

9.   B
bighampton, the president of the largest class, has the biggest heart.

10.   M   D   G   J   L
mandy, diane, gene, and james belong to a lovely family in louisiana.

11.   B   S   C   D
bighampton went around with santa claus on december twenty-fourth.

12.   I C   B   S
in canada, bighampton found it slightly cool on santa's sleigh.

13.   S   A   N   A   E   A
santa visited asia, north america, europe, and australia in about three hours on
  C   E
christmas eve.

14.   B   B   S F
bighampton flew the sleigh from boston to san francisco in the twinkling of an
eye.

15.   W   B   S   T
when they left boston, santa shouted, "this is the home of the best hockey team
of all time."

77. Identifying Kinds of Sentences

1. ! exclamatory (or . imperative)
2. ? interrogative
3. ! exclamatory
4. . declarative
5. . declarative
6. ! exclamatory (or . imperative)
7. ? interrogative
8. . declarative
9. ? interrogative
10. ! exclamatory

78. Punctuation

No answers required.

79. Showing Separate and Joint Possession

1. Bill's and Larry's dogs are gentle and kind.
2. Esther admired Alan and Wanda's house.
3. Esther and her husband's farm is wonderful.
4. Marlene's and her friend Carol's drawings have a professional touch.
5. Yesterday we went to Peter's and Mary's homes.
6. Maggie and her sister's truck was full.
7. The doctor's and the staff's responses were terrific.
8. Marlene's and Carol's new cars both had bad dents.
9. We visited the display at Johnson and Wilson's market.
10. Why did you not want Smith and Henry's new Ferrari?

80. Possessive Singular and Possessive Plural

POSSESSIVE SINGULAR	POSSESSIVE PLURAL
2. elephant's trunk	elephants' trunks
3. hive's queen	hives' queens
4. cowgirl's hat	cowgirls' hats
5. tiger's tail	tigers' tails
6. secretary's desk	secretaries' desks
7. mother-in-law's cane	mothers-in-laws' canes
8. Esther's last name	Esthers' last names
9. orange's flavor	oranges' flavors
10. wife's paycheck	wives' paychecks
11. box's lid	boxes' lids
12. knife's blade	knives' blades
13. doctor's bill	doctors' bills
14. nurse's uniform	nurses' uniforms
15. patient's gown	patients' gowns

81. "Person" of Nouns

1. first	6. third	11. third
2. third	7. second	12. third
3. third	8. third	13. first
4. second	9. third	14. third
5. third	10. third	15. first

82. Where Are the Vowels?

One day Humpty Dumpty decided to do some serious sitting.

His mom said, "You can't do serious sitting. You're too rounded on the bottom. Son, you're just too oval."

"Don't worry about me, Mom; I'm a teenager now, and I don't need to listen to old scrambled ideas," he retorted proudly.

With that the confident Humpty went off to find a serious sitting adventure.

At first he tried several places. He was too wide to sit on a skateboard or scooter and the video parlor was just too noisy. Finally, while walking along and wondering why his parents would name a kid Humpty in the first place, he spied the perfect spot. It was a stone wall.

"Ah, ha!" he blurted. "Let the serious sitting adventure begin." As he nestled down on top of the wall, he could see somebody coming. Leaning forward to see and not aware he was losing his grip, he said, "Hi, king's horses and king's men." Suddenly, oops . . . and the rest is history.

83. Capitalization Skills

Several years ago little Miss Muffet was said to have sat on a tuffet eating curds and whey. Breanna Buckingham told Jamalia Sousa in Boston that curds and whey were the solid and watery parts of milk. A mystery remains, however, as to what a tuffet is. Bighampton Butler Jones from Scranton thinks it is a toadstool, but he is not sure. No dictionary, not even the famous <u>Peterson's Dictionary</u>, has the definition of a tuffet. Perhaps we should hire the Zip Detective Service to solve the mystery. The whole world wants to have the answer to this burning question, "What is a tuffet?"

Extra Credit Question: A tuffet is a tuft of grass or a low stool.

84. Verb Tenses: Part One

1. past	7. past	13. past
2. future	8. present	14. past
3. past	9. future	15. future
4. present	10. present	16. present
5. present	11. future	17. past
6. present	12. present	18. past

85. Verb Tenses: Part Two

1. past	9. future	16. future
2. future	10. present	17. present
3. past	11. future	18. past
4. present	12. present	19. future
5. present	13. past	20. past
6. present	14. future	21. present
7. past	15. past	22. past
8. present		

86. Using Capitals Properly

       C

2. canada is a large and cold country with nice warm people.

     M   J   J   M   S

3. mike saw jamalia at the johnson market on saturday.

     B   B   S   C   V

4. bighampton took breanna to see *space cadets from venus* at the theatre.

     S   B

5. sonia really liked bighampton in the school play.

     B   L A

6. breanna was jealous of this new girl from los alamos.

     A   K   M   M

7. aunt kathy moved here from malta, montana.

     C   W   B   B M

8. cody, wyoming has a wonderful buffalo bill museum.

     L   J   M   S   M   Y   N

9. last week jamalia and mike went hiking on sugar mountain in yoho national
park.

     O S   B   B   J   B   A

10. on saturday bighampton butler jones flew to boise with akira.

     B   F   M   W

11. breanna works at the flamingo motel as a chambermaid after school on wednesdays.

     M B   A   S   P

12. miss bartel, the principal of alexander school, is going to poughkeepsie.

87. Baseball Vowel Strikeout

R	E	C	O	R	D	S	R	B	P	X	R	W	X	M	B	F	T
C	S	P	E	T	M	N	D	W	A	E	P	G	L	O	V	E	F
N	M	F	I	E	L	D	E	R	T	T	X	V	P	U	W	L	A
V	A	O	D	T	C	S	P	T	O	U	T	M	N	N	W	I	S
S	S	U	O	D	C	M	I	S	L	I	D	E	R	D	M	N	T
T	T	L	U	D	F	H	O	M	E	R	U	N	R	R	M	E	B
E	R	B	B	B	A	S	E	F	F	P	Q	P	W	U	M	D	A
A	I	A	L	R	T	V	P	C	D	F	R	B	I	N	N	R	L
L	K	L	E	M	M	D	I	A	M	O	N	D	M	N	P	I	L
T	E	L	M	J	D	R	C	J	P	L	A	M	L	E	L	V	R
N	P	B	H	O	M	E	P	L	A	T	E	S	T	R	R	E	T
F	L	Y	B	A	L	L	K	N	S	D	F	R	P	B	U	N	T

88. Using and Understanding Suffixes

2. treatable, liveable (livable), colorable, reasonable, remarkable
3. wonderful, helpful, hopeful, playful, thankful
4. powerless, hopeless, painless, careless, useless
5. foolish, selfish, fiendish, feverish, childish
6. sporty, jaunty, faulty, curly, filthy
7. abatement, refreshment, pronouncement, abandonment, enjoyment
8. drunken, heighten, lessen, soften, harden
9. combative, destructive, corrective, objective, selective
10. flying, holding, fighting, thinking, feeling

89. Using and Understanding Prefixes

2. return, replace, retired, removed, rebuilt
3. income, injustice, inland, inoperable, inorganic
4. antisocial, antifreeze, antiballistic, antibody, anticlimax
5. anytime, anyplace, anyone, anything, anyway
6. define, defile, dethrone, dehumidify, defame
7. transfigure, transfix, transaction, transatlantic, transcribe
8. misplace, misname, misfortune, misgiving, mislead
9. interchange, interlock, intercollegiate, intercontinental, intergalactic
10. exact, extradition, exchange, exclaim, extraction

90. Thou Shalt Enjoy This Vowelless Puzzle

S	V	R	C	B	Q	B	O	U	L	D	E	R	D	F	N	M	C	R
T	S	E	P	A	R	A	T	I	S	T	N	M	K	L	X	F	O	T
R	P	A	E	N	G	L	A	N	D	H	O	L	L	A	N	D	L	M
A	E	P	T	S	A	N	I	T	A	R	Y	F	L	E	D	J	O	P
N	E	U	C	N	T	B	K	V	O	Y	A	G	E	T	Z	M	N	V
G	D	R	H	B	T	J	P	T	L	G	R	I	M	W	P	N	I	M
E	W	I	W	R	L	S	R	R	P	E	R	S	U	A	D	E	S	H
R	E	T	R	V	G	V	E	G	P	L	Y	M	O	U	T	H	T	G
S	L	A	C	C	S	W	V	T	S	C	O	N	D	E	M	N	E	D
P	L	N	H	R	T	V	A	N	B	T	M	K	V	L	P	T	X	W
C	U	S	T	O	M	S	C	E	G	C	O	M	P	A	C	T	T	R
D	I	S	E	A	S	E	Y	A	S	T	H	C	J	O	E	N	T	T
M	A	Y	F	L	O	W	E	R	R	V	W	B	K	P	R	Q	P	W

SECTION 4

91. Finding Words from Clues and Scrambles

1. a(s)k
2. arrogan(t)
3. assa(u)lt
4. bran(d)
5. braz(e)n
6. broade(n)
7. dain(t)y
8. dam(s)el
9. desper(a)do
10. ea(r)drum
11. dwindl(e)
12. extra(v)agant
13. h(e)n
14. falte(r)
15. fantas(y)
16. farfet(c)hed
17. fam(o)us
18. f(o)liage
19. hi(l)arious

Circled letters spell: Students are very cool.

92. Building a Limerick

Answers will vary.

93. Understanding Double Negatives

1. "I never have any fun," said Figgy.
2. I don't have any of those green elephants. (or) I have none of those green elephants.
3. I have hardly started my essay.
4. I can't find anything to do. (or) I can find nothing to do.
5. I have never had such a rare steak.
6. I don't have any. (or) I have none.
7. Have you ever had such a horse as that?
8. Elephants are never small.
9. She wasn't anywhere today. (or) She was nowhere today.
10. Joe has never landed a space shuttle.

94. Placing Words in Context

Benny Smith was a very <u>poor</u> young man. He never had any <u>money</u> for candy or other goodies that he so much desired. His mother was a <u>single</u> parent who worked at two jobs just to make <u>ends</u> meet.

Benny had to look after himself and his little <u>sister</u> after school. Some people called him a <u>latchkey</u> kid. This didn't bother Benny because he had a <u>dream</u>. He was going to play <u>basketball</u> when he grew up. Already he was able to play with the high school students in the yard behind the <u>tenement</u> even though he was <u>thirteen</u>.

Benny knew he had to work hard to break the cycle of <u>poverty</u>. One thing he knew to do was to eat the <u>right</u> foods. If he was to <u>grow</u> tall enough, he had to have the proper <u>nutrition</u>. His mom made very <u>effort</u> to feed Benny and his eight-year-old sister <u>properly</u>.

One day Benny saw that he was a <u>better</u> player than the best high school <u>stu-dent</u>. With more hard <u>work</u> and proper eating habits, Benny <u>grew</u> to be seven feet two inches by the time he finished high school. <u>Major</u> league scouts were all after him to sign a contract.

His <u>clean</u> life made the difference. Now, Benny is a top player in the <u>NBA</u> and a fine example to all kids who have to do it the <u>hard</u> way.

95. Using Words Correctly

1. surely	6. leave	11. an
2. written	7. driven	12. written
3. really	8. Let	13. these *or* those
4. wore	9. writing	14. Those
5. This	10. rode	15. These

96. The Language Enrichment Chart

Possible related words:

1. action, electronic, games	9. enormous, huge, large
2. books, homework, ruler	10. archangel, cherub, heavenly
3. appetite, gobble, hungry	11. irk, mad, rage
4. bang, echo, loud	12. observe, sight, view
5. race, scurry, travel	13. door, gate, window
6. affection, fondness, liking	14. flight, flow, gallop
7. peewee, small, tiny	15. humanity, mankind, person
8. car, truck, wagon	

97. Using Distinctive or Character Words in Context

Possible answers:

okay—marvelous, nifty, fantastic, vibrant	*thought*—contemplated
happy—jolly	*win*—triumph
bad—nasty, overbearing	*large*—overbearing, overpowering
an ill feeling—jitters, shakes	*active*—agile, nimble, vibrant
run—scamper	*strength*—power, energy
harmful—nasty, overbearing, overpowering	*bad animal*—ogre, troll, beast
shock—jolt	*pot*—cauldron
wonderful—marvelous, fantastic, glorious	*feeling bad about it*—remorse, regret

98. Alphabetizing

1. promote, prompt, prone, proof, prop, proper
2. rock, rod, rogue, roll, romance, romp
3. suffix, sugar, suggest, suit, sulk, summit
4. approve, aquatic, arbor, arch, arena, arise
5. creep, crest, crew, crime, crisis, crooked
6. rise, risk, rival, river, road, roast
7. shot, shout, show, shrewd, shrine, shrivel
8. too, top, topic, torch, toss, total
9. vacant, vacate, vacation, vagabond, vague, vain
10. zany, zeal, zealot, zenith, zero, zest

99. Alphabetical Sports and Activities

1. badminton
2. band
3. basketball
4. Bible study
5. Camera Club
6. cheerleading
7. debating
8. drama
9. football
10. gymnastics
11. high jump
12. ice hockey
13. javelin
14. oratory
15. shot put
16. skipping
17. swimming
18. table tennis
19. tennis
20. tiddly winks
21. track
22. volleyball
23. weight lifting
24. wrestling

100. Organizing by Alphabetizing

1. (1) Kallback
   (2) Tilford
   (1) Anthony
   (1) Aulinger
   (2) Zizmarthy
   (1) Brenna
   (1) Hall
   (1) Heffernan
   (1) Johnson
   (2) Lengyel
   (2) Oke
   (2) Parent
   (2) Poulin
   (2) Robinson
   (2) Tegart
   (2) Waldner
   (1) Elgert
   (2) Stade

2. (9) Wilson
   (8) Smith
   (1) Bighampton
   (2) Carpentier
   (7) Ruberry
   (4) King
   (3) Dament
   (5) McCallum
   (6) Moir

101. Lazy Language Puzzle

W	B	C	A	N	T	Y	O	U	R	E	D	S	T	E
A	W	J	I	W	D	I	D	Y	O	U	B	M	N	I
N	O	W	O	N	T	Y	O	U	P	N	R	W	S	U
T	U	R	V	Y	P	C	C	O	M	E	H	E	R	E
T	L	D	S	V	I	H	V	B	N	J	A	O	K	L
O	D	W	R	E	G	O	T	T	O	U	V	M	T	G
B	Y	B	N	I	E	I	L	E	T	M	E	M	U	O
E	O	P	V	U	T	D	U	N	B	U	T	I	L	T
G	U	E	C	H	O	W	A	R	E	Y	O	U	T	Y
H	M	I	U	S	U	D	W	H	A	T	S	U	P	O
E	I	D	O	N	T	K	N	O	W	V	W	R	T	U

102. Spelling Civil War Battles: Part One

```
        C                          G E T T Y S B U R G
        H                                  H
        A                                  I
        T                                  L
        T                                  O
F R A N K L I N                            H
        N
        O
        O
        G
        A


              V                              P
              I                              E
              C                              R
              K                              R
P E T E R S B U R G        S P O T S Y L V A N I A
              S                              I
              B                              L
              U                              L
              R                              E
              G
```

103. Spelling Civil War Battles: Part Two

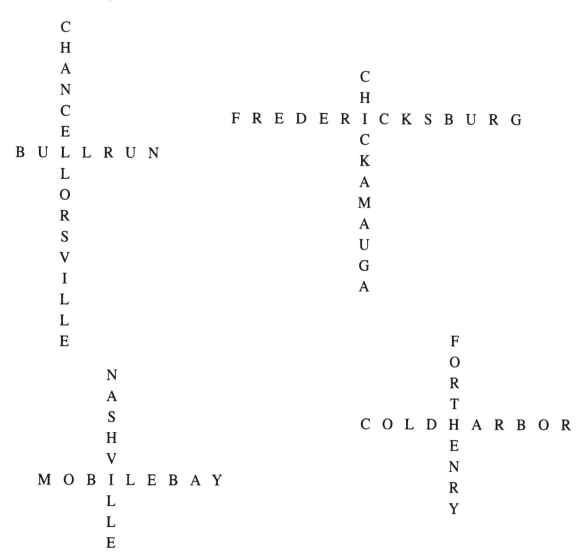

104. *Titanic* Words and Expressions

1. water-tight compartments
2. *Carpathia*
3. davits
4. iceberg
5. unsinkable
6. tonnage
7. maiden voyage
8. White Star Line
9. Southampton
10. women and children first
11. the bridge
12. Titan
13. life jacket
14. steerage
15. four

105. Vocabulary Development with President Lincoln

1. bin
2. liar
3. brim
4. Main
5. brain
6. lab
7. lion
8. mama
9. rabbi
10. coin
11. Cobra
12. March
13. ribbon
14. banana
15. hail
16. mall
17. barn
18. hill
19. corn
20. hair
21. cool
22. him
23. limo
24. ram
25. calm

106. "F"-Sounding Words with No "F"

1. telephone
2. phonograph
3. nephew
4. pharaoh
5. photograph
6. rough
7. telegraph
8. autograph
9. orphan
10. enough
11. phrenology
12. graph
13. photosyn-
   thesis
14. physique
15. cough
16. phlebitis
17. Philip
18. pharmacist
19. tough
20. phobia

107. Strange and Unusual "A" Words

1. abreast
2. acromegaly
3. addled
4. adieu
5. Aeolus
6. aerie
7. aegis
8. affidavit
9. Aesop
10. agog
11. aide-de-camp
12. alewife
13. anthropo-
   morphic
14. apologist
15. arbitrate
16. auspicious
17. azalea
18. azure
19. aphasia
20. aphelia

108. Strange and Unusual "H" Words

1. hocus-pocus
2. haggis
3. haberdasher
4. hackneyed
5. hagfish
6. harpsichord
7. head cheese
8. hoarfrost
9. harum-
   scarum
10. haversack
11. heehaw
12. hedgehog
13. hansom
14. herpetology
15. hogshead
16. hobnob
17. hogwash
18. hoity-toity
19. huggermugger
20. hurdy-gurdy

109. Strange and Unusual "M" Words

1. mausoleum
2. membrane
3. mayhem
4. megalomania
5. meow
6. meringue
7. Minotaur
8. mollycoddle
9. monkey
   wrench
10. moo
11. moot court
12. mukluk
13. mucilage
14. modus
   operandi
15. mud puppy
16. musketeer
17. myrrh
18. mediocre
19. magnolia
20. mail

110. Strange and Unusual "W" Words

1. Waterloo
2. waggish
3. wax myrtle
4. wallaby
5. white-livered
6. wampum
7. woad
8. wapiti
9. wastrel
10. waif
11. weft
12. wherry
13. wiglet
14. wildebeest
15. wraith
16. widow's mite
17. wadi
18. windlass
19. woebegone
20. wanigan

111. U.S.A. Spelling Puzzle

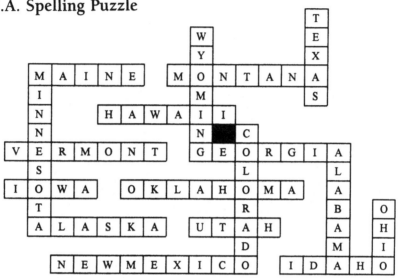

112. World Spelling Puzzle

113. The Spelling Cube

Answers will vary.

SECTION 5

114. The Phobia Report: Part One

1. Triskaidekaphobia
2. Hematophobia
3. Climacophobia
4. Chionophobia
5. Pantrophobia
6. Hylophobia
7. Ophidiophobia
8. Ailurophobia
9. Doraphobia
10. Cremnophobia

115. The Phobia Report: Part Two

1. Ochlophobia
2. Melissophobia
3. Cherophobia
4. Bacillophobia
5. Gephyrophobia
6. Domatophobia
7. Odynophobia
8. Kinesophobia
9. Monophobia
10. Achluophobia

116. Working and Speaking Positively

Answers may vary:

Jack and Jill were two <u>good</u> students at Beaumont Hill High School. They wanted to do something <u>exciting</u> that would fill their day with <u>thrills</u>.

"Let's go fetch a pail of water," Jill said <u>happily</u>. "It will be <u>fantastic</u>," she continued.

"Big deal," Jack retorted, "look at my crown. I'm already king of our classroom. What could be more <u>wonderful</u> than that? Besides, what's so great about a pail of water?"

"There's a big <u>prize</u> for the person with the fullest pail of water."

"Sounds strange to me, but for a serious <u>prize</u> I will do it," he said in <u>anticipation</u>.

Soon Jack and Jill were advancing up Beaumont Hill. Jack kept looking around at the <u>spectacular</u> view and adjusting the crown of which he was so <u>proud</u>.

"Come on, Jack," Jill <u>encouraged</u>. "We want to be the <u>winners</u>."

They soon <u>conquered</u> the hill and filled their pail with water.

Suddenly Jack yelled, "Oops."

All Jill could see was Jack tumbling end over end down Beaumont Hill. Frightened, Jill ran after him, still trying her <u>best</u> to carry her pail. <u>Miraculously</u> she did not spill a drop. She soon arrived at the bottom where Jack lay in a heap.

"How do you expect us to have <u>good</u> fortune and be a <u>success</u> if you keep abandoning me," she said sternly.

"Look at my <u>pretty</u> crown," Jack groaned, "it's broken to pieces. I thought you were supposed to come tumbling after me."

"I did give it some thought but saw no reason to do it," Jill replied, as she collected her winnings for having the <u>fullest</u> pail of water.

117. Mark Twain Quotes

1. D   4. F
2. B   5. E
3. C   6. A

118. Not the Same As . . .

Answers will vary.

119. Oxymorons Made Easy: Part One

Answers will vary.

120. Oxymorons Made Easy: Part Two

Answers will vary.

121. Seeing Both Sides of a Rule

Answers will vary.

122. Rhyming Ratios

2. frown   7. birth   12. creep   17. tough
3. shut   8. run, from   13. bare   18. sew
4. caress, bless 9. near   14. park   19. daughter
5. bold   10. nose   15. snappy   20. take
6. found   11. bad   16. mean

The relationship of the "is to" words is they are all antonyms (word opposites) of each other.

123. Finding Mistakes

1. None of the boys got their homework done.
2. Those boys need a talking to.
3. Bighampton was the worst.
4. Vinny set Gina down after the cheerleading routine.
5. Bighampton says he lost his identification in a flood.
6. Those pigs were in their sty.
7. Vinny doesn't like pigs.
8. Ideas were Vinny's weakest point.
9. Stuff is written up slowly.
10. Vinny is a pal of his.
11. You are all from the South.
12. She could have gone to the South, too.

124. Building a Quote Using Video-Game Words

1. Heat	7. Opponent	13. Crash	19. Tournament
2. Launch	8. Hammer	14. Storm	20. Wacky
3. Rogue	9. Metal	15. Gladiator	21. Fortress
4. Zone	10. Image	16. Unreal	22. Raven
5. Dream	11. Clutch	17. Force	23. Conquest
6. Raider	12. Gaming	18. Controller	

Quote: "The earth laughs in flowers," e e cummings

125. Correct Context Usage

Once upon a time there were two wonderful students named Hansel and Gretel. They had a day off from the Woodlands Middle School, so they decided to explore the forest nearby. ~~Hansel was at the doctor the day of the school video game tournament.~~

Both Hansel and Gretel enjoyed exploring the woods because they loved nature. ~~Gretel's dad had a flat tire on his pickup truck.~~ They could smell the pine and fir trees as they got near the forest. It was so inviting that they went deep into the forest. ~~Hansel's dog "Nero" was taken to the vet on Wednesday.~~ "Look at all the squirrels and chipmunks," Hansel blurted as he skipped down the forest path.

~~"I went to the skateboard park," replied Gretel.~~

"This is strange," they both cried at once when they saw a tasty candy-covered cottage in the forest.

"Welcome here," a friendly, but ugly, witch stated. ~~"I went for a ride in my car," she said.~~

"I'll have a taste of your house," Hansel replied. They entered the candy house of the friendly, but ugly, witch. The witch then thrust them into her oven and cackled, "Ah, ha, perhaps after this they will not trust strangers."

Suddenly Hansel and Gretel burst from the oven and fled from the candy house and the forest.

~~Back in school, Hansel said to Gretel, "We should e-mail Uncle Gene."~~

126. Using Sentences to Show Relationships

Answers will vary.

127. Scary Things: Part One

Answers will vary.

128. Scary Things: Part Two

Answers will vary.

129. How One Thing Is Like Another: Part One

Answers will vary.

130. How One Thing Is Like Another: Part Two
Answers will vary.

131. How One Thing Is Different from Another: Part One
Answers will vary.

132. How One Thing Is Different from Another: Part Two
Answers will vary.

133. Brainstorming
Answers will vary.

134. Following Directions

1. A. chase, gold
   B. gorilla, gossip
   C. naval, muddy
   D. ship

2. A. free spending, gold
   B. eternity, musician
   C. description, nab
   D. shock, shiver

3. A. Queen, venom
   B. musician, gorilla, excellent
   C. naval, myth
   D. active, profit

4. A. produce, chase
   B. gossip, haunt
   C. nab, muddy
   D. shock, profit

135. Filling in the Verbs
Possible answers:

1. went
2. drove, see
3. tied
4. was
5. gawked
6. ran
7. had, said
8. think
9. tell, was
10. name, queried, laughed

SECTION 6

136. What's the Time?

1. future	6. year	11. 2	16. February 29
2. past	7. 12	12. 14	17. answer varies
3. present	8. 7	13. answer varies	18. answer varies
4. yesterday	9. 24	14. answer varies	19. 10
5. tomorrow	10. clock (or watch)	15. 366	20. 100

137. Timelines

Answers will vary.

138. Organizing Your Schedule

Answers will vary. Here is a sample:

	MONDAY	TUESDAY	WEDNESDAY	THURSDAY	FRIDAY
8 A.M. 9 A.M.	Get out	of bed,	prepare and	walk	to school
9 A.M. 10 A.M.	Science	Study in library	Student	Math	History Essay Writing
10 A.M. 11 A.M.	Exam	Spare	Junior Business	Exam	Spare
11 A.M. 12 Noon	Volleyball Practice	Volleyball Practice	Meeting	Volleyball Practice	Volleyball Practice
12 Noon 1 P.M.	Lunch	Lunch	Lunch	Lunch	Lunch
1 P.M. 2 P.M.	Science	School	Debating	Debating	Band
2 P.M. 3 P.M.	Project Meeting	Choir	Club	Club	Practice

139. Understanding Shared Ideas/Concepts: Part One

Possible answers:

1. tiredness	6. art	11. dog
2. weather	7. animals	12. communication
3. teeth	8. car (or truck)	13. cat
4. colors	9. hardness	14. wedding
5. buying	10. stopping	15. smartness

140. Understanding Shared Ideas/Concepts: Part Two
Possible answers:

1. Halloween
2. baseball
3. space
4. farming
5. school
6. science
7. richness
8. style
9. video games
10. happiness
11. heroes
12. choosing
13. football
14. computer
15. house

141. Understanding Shared Ideas/Concepts: Part Three
Possible answers:

1. makeup
2. hair
3. telephone
4. jewelry
5. shoes
6. sweaters
7. ladies' apparel/ clothes
8. chocolate
9. warm-weather clothing
10. cold-weather clothing
11. hobbies
12. sports or recreation
13. careers
14. bags or purses
15. headgear or hats

142. Getting Rid of Boring Verbs: Part One
Answers will vary. Here are suggestions:

1. waddled
2. left
3. gawked
4. blurted
5. maneuvered
6. retailed
7. cranked up
8. smashed
9. cooed
10. punched
11. bounded
12. plopped
13. converse
14. spring
15. leap

143. Getting Rid of Boring Verbs: Part Two
Answers will vary. Here are suggestions:

1. desiring
2. romped
3. spied
4. distressed
5. leaped
6. alerted
7. remain, tend to be
8. traveled
9. sauntered
10. dropped
11. bounded, slammed
12. discover
13. arrived, searched
14. sense
15. recovered

144. Emergency Response
Answers will vary.

145. Understanding Clichés and Idioms: Part One

1. C	5. H
2. E	6. D
3. F	7. A
4. G	8. B

146. Understanding Clichés and Idioms: Part Two

1. F	5. G
2. D	6. H
3. A	7. B
4. E	8. C

147. Matching Idioms and Clichés to Their Meanings: Part One

T	B	K	I
E	C	G	N
S	Q	H	O
J	D	L	P
R	F	M	A

148. Matching Idioms and Clichés to Their Meanings: Part Two

R	B	T	I
S	O	F	P
L	C	G	J
M	D	A	K
N	E	H	Q

149. Presidential Match

13	4	24	22	12
20	2	3	15	18
1	6	17	7	16
9	25	5	8	14 or 19
10	11	23	14 or 19	21

150. Spelling Names of U.S. States and Presidents from Clues

1. Fillmore
2. Massachusetts
3. North Carolina
4. Iowa
5. Harding
6. Coolidge
7. New Jersey
8. Kentucky
9. Colorado
10. Montana
11. Carter
12. Bush
13. Mississippi
14. Arkansas
15. Illinois
16. Washington
17. Idaho
18. Cleveland
19. Rutherford
20. Oklahoma
21. Indiana
22. Arthur
23. Madison
24. Adams

151. Spelling U.S. Cities from Clues

1. Wallawalla, WA
2. Roseburg, OR
3. Indianapolis, IN
4. Madison, WI
5. Dayton, OH
6. Los Angeles, CA
7. Carson City, NV
8. Salt Lake City, UT
9. Winslow, AZ
10. Redbird, WY
11. Norfolk, VA
12. Cleveland, OH
13. Louisville, KY
14. Memphis, TN
15. Boston, MA
16. Baltimore, MD
17. Binghamton, NY
18. Grand Forks, ND
19. Bowling Green, KY
20. Pittsburgh, PH
21. Roswell, NM
22. Tampa, FL
23. New Orleans, LA
24. Little Rock, AR
25. Grand Rapids, MI
26. Omaha, NE
27. Denver, CO
28. New Haven, CT
29. Providence, RI
30. Colorado Spring, CO
31. Bakersfield, CA
32. Reno, NV
33. Brookhaven, MS
34. Kissimmee, FL
35. Mobile, AL
36. Fort Worth, TX

152. What Would You Do If . . . : Part One
Answers will vary.

153. What Would You Do If . . . : Part Two
Answers will vary.

154. The People Puzzle
Possible answers:

1. David is Ruth's husband.
2. Tony is George and Kathy's son.
3. Kathy is not related to David and Ruth.
4. Ben is Maria's son-in-law.
5. George and Ben are brothers-in-law.
6. Ben is Henry's son-in-law.
7. Jack is Frieda's brother.
8. Karrie is Christa's sister-in-law.
9. Tony is Kathy's son.
10. Henry and Maria are husband and wife.
11. Margaret is Karrie's sister.
12. Tony is Kevin's brother-in-law.
13. Olaf and Eva are Kevin's uncle and aunt.
14. Henry is Christa's grandfather.
15. Shadow and George are not related.

155. Reasoning from Context

1. A baby was found in a cradle on a treetop.

2–8. Answers will vary.

156. Word Completions: Part One

SET A

1. student	6. film	11. serve
2. navigator	7. fight	12. quiet
3. crocodile	8. jingle	13. stow
4. behavior	9. zombie	14. ready
5. chicken	10. explain	

SET B

1. zigzag	6. hidden	11. tow
2. complete	7. jacket	12. running
3. trouble	8. quickly	13. exactly
4. decide	9. monkey	14. why
5. lovely	10. first	

157. Word Completions: Part Two

SET A

1. question	6. examine	11. define
2. forget	7. zero	12. bookcase
3. jargon	8. lucky	13. hug
4. linoleum	9. wave	14. cupcake
5. happy	10. sugar	

SET B

1. zany	6. civilization	11. jewelry
2. instrument	7. bureaucracy	12. handsome
3. insubordinate	8. volatile	13. quirk
4. foreground	9. formation	14. fix
5. decrease	10. jalopy	

158. You Should . . . : Part One

Answers will vary.

159. You Should . . . : Part Two

Answers will vary.

160. You Should . . . : Part Three
Answers will vary.

161. The Odd One Out

1. airplane
2. chicken
3. never
4. drown
5. elephant
6. basement
7. hubcap
8. fear
9. wastebasket
10. flight
11. lazy
12. color
13. happy
14. love
15. integrity
16. scarf
17. outmoded
18. empty
19. retain
20. dud
21. seat
22. lose
23. joy
24. careless
25. terrible

SECTION 7

162. Creative Writing with Strange Facts: Part One
Answers will vary.

163. Creative Writing with Strange Facts: Part Two
Answers will vary.

164. Creative Alien Writing
Answers will vary.

165. Recognizing and Making Sentences
Possible answers:

1. Joe and the dumptruck worked all day.
3. The electronic magazine featured "Gobomonster" and his friends.
6. Bighampton's car is old, green, and fast.
7. The days of flower power and hippies ended as styles changed.
8. Bighampton's antique hot rod will often backfire.
9. Many fine video games can be rented from the corner store.
10. There are so many wonderful monsters at the movies.
11. The famous author wrote two stories about three award-winning teachers.

166. Avoiding Run-on Sentences: Part One
Answers will vary. Here is one possible answer:

Once upon a time a chicken named Henrietta was very upset because she did not know why the sky was blue. She became very anxious to find out, so she sought out an intelligent character named Foxy McGillicutty who seemed to "know it all." When she found him, she inquired why the sky was blue. Foxy McGillicutty was intelligent all right, as well as sly and smooth. He convinced Henrietta that the only real way to tell why the sky was blue was to see it from the inside of his huge cooking kettle which was conveniently hung over a large fire. Foxy convinced her that the heat would give her new insights into this question. Henrietta didn't think twice, so she hopped in. It is not known if Henrietta found out why the sky was blue, but for sure, she doesn't have to be anxious about it anymore. However, Foxy did gain weight!

167. Avoiding Run-on Sentences: Part Two
Answers will vary. Here is one possible answer:

There was a bright little girl named Mary who wanted to visit The Big Buster Video Game Station. She had one problem, however. It bothered her because she didn't know what to do. Her little lamb kept following her into the establishment and butting the other players. The owners were upset. The video station was no place for a lamb, even though the lamb, Butsy Wutsy, was cute. Mary had to take her home where she belonged. When Mary returned, The Big Buster Video Station was closed for the day.

168. Logical Responses: Part One

Answers will vary.

169. Logical Responses: Part Two

Answers will vary.

170. One Famous Person Writes to Another: Part One

Answers will vary.

171. One Famous Person Writes to Another: Part Two

Answers will vary.

172. Doubling the Creativity

Answers will vary.

173. Constructing Sentences with Keywords

Answers will vary. *What did you notice about the words?*
Two words in each set are opposites.

174. Writing about a Fashion Show

Answers will vary.

175. Writing about a Video Game

Answers will vary.

176. This Is No Accident!

Answers will vary. Here are some possible answers:

1. Bighampton stubbed his toe by accident when the car stopped suddenly.
2. While driving her car, Bree stopped suddenly and saw the accident.
3. The stop sign was finally placed at the corner where the accident occurred.
4. When taking driving lessons, you must watch for other cars so you can avoid an accident.
5. Bighampton moaned all night after hurting his big toe by accident.
6. Breanna yelled, "Watch out, or you will have an accident!"
7. She had an accident at the supermarket.
8. Molly had a nice day, free from accidents.
9. Breanna thinks girls have less accidents when driving than boys do.
10. The woman has driven for years without an accident.

177. Changing the Order of a Sentence

1. With wonderful skill drove the two students.
2. To the back of the room walked Jamalia.
3. Into the hall ran Breanna.

4. Beside the fence galloped Akira.

5. To the dance had come a muscular man named Tony.

6. Out the door scurried Bighampton.

7. On the stage stood the powerful man.

8. Louder and louder talked Sunshine and Tony.

178. Using Correct Language

Answers may vary. Here are suggestions:

1. Those dogs were all badly behaved.

2. I could hardly control them.

3. They lay in their cages a time long.

4. "Bighampton, please let me see those puppies."

5. "I don't have any dog food," Reanna blurted.

6. Horizon and I think we can teach them some tricks.

7. I bought a video game with great graphics from this kid.

8. That dog isn't any different from the mutt I have.   or   That dog is no different from my mutt.

9. My brother Bartholomew ran away and began to cry.

10. I trained my dog to sit down when eating.

179. Newspaper Headlines: Part One

Answers will vary.

180. Newspaper Headlines: Part Two

Answers will vary.

181. Applying for a Loan

Answers will vary.

182. Applying for a Driver's License

Answers will vary.

183. Applying for Employment

Answers will vary.

184. Writing a Friendly Letter

1. heading, greeting, body, closing, signature

2. comma

3. comma

4. comma

5. heading

6. the name in the greeting (Beanie)

7. Dear

8. the second word

185. Designing a Bicycle Seat

Answers will vary.

186. Designing a Hot Rod

Answers will vary.

187. I Say the Earth Is Flat

Answers will vary.

188. Creating an Ad

Answers will vary.

189. Opening and Closing a Paragraph

Answers will vary.

190. Writing Paragraphs

Once upon a time, long ago and far away (actually it was last year in Poughkeepsie), a cow, a cat, a plate, and a spoon all had the same goal. They wanted more happiness and excitement in their lives.

"I think I'll jump over the moon," Bossy the Cow said with assurance as she looked at the sky.

Diddle Diddle the Cat stated, "That's a wonderful idea, but to have long-lasting excitement, I will learn to play the fiddle."

The Plate and the Spoon both said they wanted more contentment in their lives and to not be thought of as just utensils!

"It can't be done," Buster the Dog criticized. "You are all foolish," he blurted as he laughed at them.

After several attempts Bossy finally succeeded and earned everlasting fame in a nursery rhyme. Buster often made fun of Diddle Diddle as he practiced many hours on the fiddle. This made Diddle Diddle's work long and hard but eventually he too succeeded and became an international star. Buster really barked nasty things at Heather the Plate and Darryl B. Spoon, but they left Buster behind as they ran away together. Heather found Darryl B. to be sweet because he was always full of sugar and Darryl thought Heather was a real dish, so they lived happily ever after in a setting of their own.

Moral of the Story: Don't let the Busters of this world step on your dreams. They are usually barking up the wrong tree.

NOTES

NOTES

NOTES

NOTES

NOTES

NOTES

NOTES

NOTES

NOTES

NOTES

NOTES